The Shorter Catechism
A Baptist Version

With Scripture Quotations From
The New King James Version

Second Edition

SIMPSON
PUBLISHING COMPANY

AVINGER, TEXAS

Simpson Publishing Company
1 South Main Street · Post Office Box 100
Avinger, Texas 75630
U.S.A.

www.simpsonpublishing.com

Scripture quotations are from *The New King James Version, The Holy Bible*
Copyright © 1983 by Thomas Nelson, Inc. Used by permission

Published 1991. Second Edition 2003

ISBN 1-881095-00-2

Printed in the United States of America

The Library of Congress has cataloged the original edition as follows:

The Shorter catechism : a Baptist version : with scripture quotations
   from the New King James Version.
      p.   cm.
   Based on the Westminster Assembly catechism, with a few
questions added and others modified to express the Baptist doctrine.
   Includes bibliographical references.
   ISBN 0-9622508-4-8
   1. Baptists—Catechisms—English. [1. Baptists—Catechisms.]
I. Simpson Publishing Company (Boonton, N.J.) II. Westminster
Assembly (1643-1652). Shorter catechism.
BX6336.S565 1991   91-21523
238'.6—dc20   CIP
                                                    AC

The Catechism with Scripture Proofs

1. What is the chief end of man?

Man's chief end is to glorify God,[1] and to enjoy Him forever.[2]

1. *1 Corinthians 10:31* Therefore, whether you eat or drink, or whatever you do, do all to the glory of God.

   Romans 11:36 For of Him and through Him and to Him are all things, to whom be glory forever. Amen.

2. *Psalm 73:25-28* Whom have I in heaven but You? And there is none upon earth that I desire besides You. [26]My flesh and my heart fail; but God is the strength of my heart and my portion forever. [27]For indeed, those who are far from You shall perish; You have destroyed all those who desert You for harlotry. [28]But it is good for me to draw near to God; I have put my trust in the Lord GOD, that I may declare all Your works.

2. What rule has God given to direct us how we may glorify and enjoy Him?

The word of God, namely the Scriptures of the Old and New Testaments,[1] is the only rule to direct us how we may glorify and enjoy Him.[2]

1. *2 Timothy 3:15-16* And that from childhood you have known the Holy Scriptures, which are able to make you wise for salvation through faith which is in Christ Jesus. [16]All Scripture is given by inspiration of God, and is profitable for doctrine, for reproof, for correction, for instruction in righteousness.

   Ephesians 2:20 Having been built on the foundation of the apostles and prophets, Jesus Christ Himself being the chief cornerstone.

2. *1 John 1:3-4* That which we have seen and heard we declare to you, that you also may have fellowship with us; and truly our fellowship is with the Father and with His Son Jesus Christ. [4]And these things we write to you that your joy may be full.

   Luke 16:29, 31 Abraham said to him, They have Moses and the prophets; let them hear them. [31]But he said to him, If they do not hear Moses and the prophets, neither will they be persuaded though one rise from the dead.

   Galatians 1:8-9 But even if we, or an angel from heaven, preach any other gospel to you than what we have preached to you, let him be accursed. [9]As we have said before, so now I say again, if anyone preaches any other gospel to you than what you have received, let him be accursed.

3. Are the Scriptures trustworthy in all that they affirm?

The Scriptures of both the Old and New Testaments, being God-breathed,[1] are infallible and inerrant in all their parts and are, therefore, trustworthy in all that they affirm concerning history, science, doctrine, ethics, religious practice, or any other topic.[2]

1. *2 Timothy 3:16* All Scripture is given by inspiration of God, and is profitable for doctrine, for reproof, for correction, for instruction in righteousness.

2. *1 Thessalonians 2:13* For this reason we also thank God without ceasing, because when you received the word of God which you heard from us, you welcomed it not as the

word of men, but as it is in truth, the word of God, which also effectively works in you who believe.

John 10:35b The Scripture cannot be broken.

4. What do the Scriptures principally teach?

The Scriptures principally teach what man is to believe concerning God, and what duty God requires of man.[1]

1. *2 Timothy 1:13* Hold fast the pattern of sound words which you have heard from me, in faith and love which are in Christ Jesus.

   2 Timothy 3:16 All Scripture is given by inspiration of God, and is profitable for doctrine, for reproof, for correction, for instruction in righteousness.

   Micah 6:8 He has shown you, O man, what is good; and what does the LORD require of you but to do justly, to love mercy, and to walk humbly with your God?

5. What is God?

God is a Spirit,[1] infinite,[2] eternal,[3] and unchangeable,[4] in His being,[5] wisdom,[6] power,[7] holiness,[8] justice, goodness, and truth.[9]

1. *John 4:24* God is Spirit, and those who worship Him must worship in spirit and truth.
2. *Job 11:7-9* Can you search out the deep things of God? Can you find out the limits of the Almighty? [8]They are higher than heaven—what can you do? Deeper than Sheol—what can you know? [9]Their measure is longer than the earth and broader than the sea.
3. *Psalm 90:2* Before the mountains were brought forth, or ever You had formed the earth and the world, even from everlasting to everlasting, You are God.
4. *James 1:17* Every good gift and every perfect gift is from above, and comes down from the Father of lights, with whom there is no variation or shadow of turning.
5. *Exodus 3:14* And God said to Moses, I AM WHO I AM. And He said, Thus you shall say to the children of Israel, I AM has sent me to you.
6. *Psalm 147:5* Great is our Lord, and mighty in power; His understanding is infinite.
7. *Job 42:2* I know that You can do everything, and that no purpose of Yours can be withheld from You.

   Revelation 4:8 And the four living creatures, each having six wings, were full of eyes around and within. And they do not rest day or night, saying: Holy, holy, holy, Lord God Almighty, Who was and is and is to come!
8. *Revelation 15:4* Who shall not fear You, O Lord, and glorify Your name? For You alone are holy. For all nations shall come and worship before You, for Your judgments have been manifested.
9. *Exodus 34:6-7* And the LORD passed before him and proclaimed, The LORD, the LORD God, merciful and gracious, longsuffering, and abounding in goodness and truth, [7]keeping mercy for thousands, forgiving iniquity and transgression and sin, by no means clearing the guilty, visiting the iniquity of the fathers upon the children and the children's children to the third and the fourth generation.

6. Are there more Gods than one?

There is but one only,[1] the living and true God.[2]

1. *Deuteronomy 6:4* Hear, O Israel: The LORD our God, the LORD is one!

2. *Jeremiah 10:10* But the Lord is the true God; He is the living God and the everlasting King. At His wrath the earth will tremble, and the nations will not be able to abide His indignation.

7. How many persons are there in the Godhead?

There are three persons in the Godhead: the Father, the Son, and the Holy Spirit;[1] and these three are one God, the same in substance, equal in power and glory.[2]

1. *Matthew 28:19* Go therefore and make disciples of all the nations, baptizing them in the name of the Father and of the Son and of the Holy Spirit.

   2 Corinthians 13:14 The grace of the Lord Jesus Christ, and the love of God, and the communion of the Holy Spirit be with you all. Amen.

2. *John 10:30* I and My Father are one.

   Acts 5:3-4 But Peter said, Ananias, why has Satan filled your heart to lie to the Holy Spirit and keep back part of the price of the land for yourself? [4]While it remained, was it not your own? And after it was sold, was it not in your own control? Why have you conceived this thing in your heart? You have not lied to men but to God.

8. What are the decrees of God?

The decrees of God are His eternal purpose, according to the counsel of His will, whereby, for His own glory, He has foreordained whatsoever comes to pass.[1]

1. *Daniel 4:35* All the inhabitants of the earth are reputed as nothing; He does according to His will in the army of heaven and among the inhabitants of the earth. No one can restrain His hand or say to Him, What have You done?

   Romans 11:36 For of Him and through Him and to Him are all things, to whom be glory forever. Amen.

   Ephesians 1:4, 11-12 Just as He chose us in Him before the foundation of the world, that we should be holy and without blame before Him in love. [11]In whom also we have obtained an inheritance, being predestined according to the purpose of Him who works all things according to the counsel of His will, [12]that we who first trusted in Christ should be to the praise of His glory.

9. How does God execute His decrees?

God executes His decrees in the works of creation[1] and providence.[2]

1. *Revelation 4:11* You are worthy, O Lord, to receive glory and honor and power; for You created all things, and by Your will they exist and were created.
2. *Ephesians 1:11* In whom also we have obtained an inheritance, being predestined according to the purpose of Him who works all things according to the counsel of His will.

10. What is the work of creation?

The work of creation is God's making all things of nothing,[1] by the word of His power,[2] in the space of six days,[3] and all very good.[4]

1. *Genesis 1:1-31* In the beginning God created the heavens and the earth....

Colossians 1:16 For by Him all things were created that are in heaven and that are on earth, visible and invisible, whether thrones or dominions or principalities or powers. All things were created through Him and for Him.

2. *Hebrews 11:3* By faith we understand that the worlds were framed by the word of God, so that the things which are seen were not made of things which are visible.

3. *Exodus 20:11* For in six days the LORD made the heavens and the earth, the sea, and all that is in them, and rested the seventh day. Therefore the LORD blessed the Sabbath day and hallowed it.

4. *Genesis 1:31* Then God saw everything that He had made, and indeed it was very good. So the evening and the morning were the sixth day.

11. How did God create man?

God created man, male and female, after His own image,[1] in knowledge,[2] righteousness,[3] and holiness,[4] with dominion over the creatures.[5]

1. *Genesis 1:27* So God created man in His own image; in the image of God He created him; male and female He created them.

2. *Colossians 3:10* And have put on the new man who is renewed in knowledge according to the image of Him who created him.

3. *Ecclesiastes 7:29* Truly, this only I have found: that God made man upright, but they have sought out many schemes.

4. *Ephesians 4:24* And that you put on the new man which was created according to God, in righteousness and true holiness.

5. *Genesis 1:26, 28* Then God said, Let Us make man in Our image, according to Our likeness; let them have dominion over the fish of the sea, over the birds of the air, and over the cattle, over all the earth and over every creeping thing that creeps on the earth. [28]Then God blessed them, and God said to them, Be fruitful and multiply; fill the earth and subdue it; have dominion over the fish of the sea, over the birds of the air, and over every living thing that moves on the earth.

12. What are God's works of providence?

God's works of providence are His most holy,[1] wise,[2] and powerful preserving[3] and governing all His creatures, and all their actions.[4]

1. *Psalm 145:17* The LORD is righteous in all His ways, gracious in all His works.

2. *Psalm 104:24* O LORD, how manifold are Your works! In wisdom You have made them all. The earth is full of Your possessions.

   Isaiah 28:29 This also comes from the LORD of hosts, who is wonderful in counsel and excellent in guidance.

3. *Hebrews 1:3* Who being the brightness of His glory and the express image of His person, and upholding all things by the word of His power, when He had by Himself purged our sins, sat down at the right hand of the Majesty on high.

   Colossians 1:17 And He is before all things, and in Him all things consist.

4. *Psalm 103:19* The LORD has established His throne in heaven, and His kingdom rules over all.

   Matthew 10:29-31 Are not two sparrows sold for a copper coin? And not one of them falls to the ground apart from your Father's will. [30]But the very hairs of your head are all numbered. [31]Do not fear therefore; you are of more value than many sparrows.

13. What was the estate wherein man was created?

Man was created[1] in an estate of sinlessness[2] and happiness[3] in which the Lord God entrusted him with care for the garden of Eden[4] and forbade him to eat from the tree of the knowledge of good and evil, upon the pain of death.[5]

1. *Genesis 2:7-8* And the LORD God formed man of the dust of the ground, and breathed into his nostrils the breath of life; and man became a living being. [8]The LORD God planted a garden eastward in Eden, and there He put the man whom He had formed.

2. *Genesis 1:31a* Then God saw everything that He had made, and indeed it was very good.
   Ecclesiastes 7:29 Truly, this only I have found: that God made man upright, but they have sought out many schemes.

3. *Genesis 2:9, 25* And out of the ground the LORD God made every tree grow that is pleasant to the sight and good for food. The tree of life was also in the midst of the garden, and the tree of the knowledge of good and evil. [25]And they were both naked, the man and his wife, and were not ashamed.

4. *Genesis 2:15* Then the LORD God took the man and put him in the garden of Eden to tend and keep it.

5. *Genesis 2:16-17* And the LORD God commanded the man, saying, Of every tree of the garden you may freely eat; [17]but of the tree of the knowledge of good and evil you shall not eat, for in the day that you eat of it you shall surely die.

14. Did our first parents continue in the estate wherein they were created?

Our first parents, being left to the freedom of their own will, fell from the estate wherein they were created, by sinning against God.[1]

1. *Genesis 3:6-8, 13, 17* So when the woman saw that the tree was good for food, that it was pleasant to the eyes, and a tree desirable to make one wise, she took of its fruit and ate. She also gave to her husband with her, and he ate. [7]Then the eyes of both of them were opened, and they knew that they were naked; and they sewed fig leaves together and made themselves coverings. [8]And they heard the sound of the LORD God walking in the garden in the cool of the day, and Adam and his wife hid themselves from the presence of the LORD God among the trees of the garden. [13]And the LORD God said to the woman, What is this you have done? And the woman said, The serpent deceived me, and I ate. [17]Then to Adam He said, Because you have heeded the voice of your wife, and have eaten from the tree of which I commanded you, saying, You shall not eat of it: cursed is the ground for your sake; in toil you shall eat of it all the days of your life.
   Ecclesiastes 7:29 Truly, this only I have found: that God made man upright, but they have sought out many schemes.

15. What is sin?

Sin is any lack of conformity unto, or transgression of, the law of God.[1]

1. *1 John 3:4* Whoever commits sin also commits lawlessness, and sin is lawlessness.

16. What was the sin whereby our first parents fell from the estate wherein they were created?

The sin whereby our first parents fell from the estate wherein they were created, was their eating the forbidden fruit.[1]

> 1. *Genesis 3:6* So when the woman saw that the tree was good for food, that it was pleasant to the eyes, and a tree desirable to make one wise, she took of its fruit and ate. She also gave to her husband with her, and he ate.
>
> *Genesis 3:9-13* Then the LORD God called to Adam and said to him, Where are you? [10]So he said, I heard Your voice in the garden, and I was afraid because I was naked; and I hid myself. [11] And He said, Who told you that you were naked? Have you eaten from the tree of which I commanded you that you should not eat? [12]Then the man said, The woman whom You gave to be with me, she gave me of the tree, and I ate. [13]And the LORD God said to the woman, What is this you have done? And the woman said, The serpent deceived me, and I ate.

17. Did all mankind fall in Adam's first transgression?

Because the prohibition regarding the forbidden fruit was given to Adam as a representative of mankind, he disobeyed not only for himself, but for his posterity; so that all mankind, descending from Adam by ordinary generation, sinned in him and fell with him in his first transgression.[1]

> 1. *Genesis 2:16-17* And the LORD God commanded the man, saying, Of every tree of the garden you may freely eat; [17]but of the tree of the knowledge of good and evil you shall not eat, for in the day that you eat of it you shall surely die.
>
> *Romans 5:12, 18-19* Therefore, just as through one man sin entered the world, and death through sin, and thus death spread to all men, because all sinned. [18]Therefore, as through one man's offense judgment came to all men, resulting in condemnation, even so through one Man's righteous act the free gift came to all men, resulting in justification of life. [19]For as by one man's disobedience many were made sinners, so also by one Man's obedience many will be made righteous.
>
> *1 Corinthians 15:21-22* For since by man came death, by Man also came the resurrection of the dead. [22]For as in Adam all die, even so in Christ all shall be made alive.

18. Into what estate did the fall bring mankind?

The fall brought mankind into an estate of sin and misery.[1]

> 1. *Romans 5:12* Therefore, just as through one man sin entered the world, and death through sin, and thus death spread to all men, because all sinned.
>
> *Genesis 3:16-19* To the woman He said: I will greatly multiply your sorrow and your conception; in pain you shall bring forth children; Your desire shall be for your husband, and he shall rule over you. [17]Then to Adam He said, Because you have heeded the voice of your wife, and have eaten from the tree of which I commanded you, saying, You shall not eat of it: Cursed is the ground for your sake; in toil you shall eat of it all the days of your life. [18]Both thorns and thistles it shall bring forth for you, and you shall eat the herb of the field. [19]In the sweat of your face you shall eat bread till you return to the ground, for out of it you were taken; for dust you are, and to dust you shall return.

19. Wherein consists the sinfulness of that estate whereinto man fell?

The sinfulness of that estate whereinto man fell, consists in the guilt of Adam's first sin,[1] the lack of original righteousness,[2] and the corruption of his whole nature,[3] which is commonly called Original Sin; together with all actual transgressions which proceed from it.[4]

1. *Romans 5:12, 19* Therefore, just as through one man sin entered the world, and death through sin, and thus death spread to all men, because all sinned. [19]For as by one man's disobedience many were made sinners, so also by one Man's obedience many will be made righteous.

2. *Ecclesiastes 7:29* Truly, this only I have found: that God made man upright, but they have sought out many schemes.

   Romans 3:10 As it is written: There is none righteous, no, not one.

3. *Ephesians 2:1-3* And you He made alive, who were dead in trespasses and sins, [2]in which you once walked according to the course of this world, according to the prince of the power of the air, the spirit who now works in the sons of disobedience, [3]among whom also we all once conducted ourselves in the lusts of our flesh, fulfilling the desires of the flesh and of the mind, and were by nature children of wrath, just as the others.

   Psalm 51:5 Behold, I was brought forth in iniquity, and in sin my mother conceived me.

4. *James 1:14-15* But each one is tempted when he is drawn away by his own desires and enticed. [15]Then, when desire has conceived, it gives birth to sin; and sin, when it is full-grown, brings forth death.

   Matthew 15:19-20a For out of the heart proceed evil thoughts, murders, adulteries, fornications, thefts, false witness, blasphemies. These are the things which defile a man.

20. What is the misery of that estate whereinto all mankind fell?

All mankind by their fall lost communion with God,[1] are under His wrath and curse,[2] and so made liable to all miseries in this life,[3] to death itself,[4] and to the pains of hell forever.[5]

1. *Genesis 3:8, 10, 24* And they heard the sound of the LORD God walking in the garden in the cool of the day, and Adam and his wife hid themselves from the presence of the LORD God among the trees of the garden. [10]So he said, I heard Your voice in the garden, and I was afraid because I was naked; and I hid myself. [24]So He drove out the man; and He placed cherubim at the east of the garden of Eden, and a flaming sword which turned every way, to guard the way to the tree of life.

2. *Ephesians 2:2-3* In which you once walked according to the course of this world, according to the prince of the power of the air, the spirit who now works in the sons of disobedience, [3]among whom also we all once conducted ourselves in the lusts of our flesh, fulfilling the desires of the flesh and of the mind, and were by nature children of wrath, just as the others.

3. *Lamentations 3:39* Why should a living man complain, a man for the punishment of his sins?

4. *Romans 6:23* For the wages of sin is death, but the gift of God is eternal life in Christ Jesus our Lord.

5. *Matthew 25:41, 46* Then He will also say to those on the left hand, Depart from Me, you cursed, into the everlasting fire prepared for the devil and his angels. ⁴⁶And these will go away into everlasting punishment, but the righteous into eternal life.

21. Did God leave all mankind to perish in the estate of sin and misery?

God having, out of His mere good pleasure, from all eternity, elected some to everlasting life,[1] did establish a way of salvation, to deliver them out of the estate of sin and misery, and to bring them into an estate of salvation by a Redeemer.[2]

1. *Ephesians 1:4* Just as He chose us in Him before the foundation of the world, that we should be holy and without blame before Him in love.

   Acts 13:48b And as many as had been appointed to eternal life believed.

2. *Romans 3:20-22* Therefore by the deeds of the law no flesh will be justified in His sight, for by the law is the knowledge of sin. ²¹But now the righteousness of God apart from the law is revealed, being witnessed by the Law and the Prophets, ²²even the righteousness of God which is through faith in Jesus Christ to all and on all who believe. For there is no difference.

   Galatians 3:21-22 Is the law then against the promises of God? Certainly not! For if there had been a law given which could have given life, truly righteousness would have been by the law. ²²But the Scripture has confined all under sin, that the promise by faith in Jesus Christ might be given to those who believe.

22. Who is the Redeemer of God's elect?

The only Redeemer of God's elect is the Lord Jesus Christ,[1] who being the eternal Son of God became man,[2] and so was, and continues to be, God and man, in two distinct natures,[3] and one person forever.[4]

1. *1 Timothy 2:5-6* For there is one God and one Mediator between God and men, the Man Christ Jesus, ⁶who gave Himself a ransom for all, to be testified in due time.

2. *John 1:14* And the Word became flesh and dwelt among us, and we beheld His glory, the glory as of the only begotten of the Father, full of grace and truth.

   Galatians 4:4 But when the fullness of the time had come, God sent forth His Son, born of a woman, born under the law.

3. *Romans 9:5* Of whom are the fathers and from whom, according to the flesh, Christ came, who is over all, the eternally blessed God. Amen.

   Luke 1:35 And the angel answered and said to her, The Holy Spirit will come upon you, and the power of the Highest will overshadow you; therefore, also, that Holy One who is to be born will be called the Son of God.

   Colossians 2:9 For in Him dwells all the fullness of the Godhead bodily.

4. *Hebrews 7:24-25* But He, because He continues forever, has an unchangeable priesthood. ²⁵Therefore He is also able to save to the uttermost those who come to God through Him, since He ever lives to make intercession for them.

23. How did Christ, being the Son of God, become man?

Christ, the Son of God, became man, by taking to Himself a true body[1] and a reasonable soul,[2] being conceived by the power of the Holy Spirit, in the womb of the Virgin Mary, and born of her,[3] yet without sin.[4]

1. *Hebrews 2:14* Inasmuch then as the children have partaken of flesh and blood, He Himself likewise shared in the same, that through death He might destroy him who had the power of death, that is, the devil.

2. *Matthew 26:38* Then He said to them, My soul is exceedingly sorrowful, even to death. Stay here and watch with Me.

3. *Luke 1:27, 31, 35, 42* To a virgin betrothed to a man whose name was Joseph, of the house of David. The virgin's name was Mary. [31]And behold, you will conceive in your womb and bring forth a Son, and shall call His name JESUS. [35]And the angel answered and said to her, The Holy Spirit will come upon you, and the power of the Highest will overshadow you; therefore, also, that Holy One who is to be born will be called the Son of God. [42]Then she spoke out with a loud voice and said, Blessed are you among women, and blessed is the fruit of your womb!

   Galatians 4:4 But when the fullness of the time had come, God sent forth His Son, born of a woman, born under the law.

4. *Hebrews 4:15* For we do not have a High Priest who cannot sympathize with our weaknesses, but was in all points tempted as we are, yet without sin.

   Hebrews 7:26 For such a High Priest was fitting for us, who is holy, harmless, undefiled, separate from sinners, and has become higher than the heavens.

24. What offices does Christ execute as the Redeemer?

Christ, as the Redeemer, executes the offices of a Prophet,[1] of a Priest,[2] and of a King,[3] both in His estate of humiliation and exaltation.

1. *Acts 3:21-22* Whom heaven must receive until the times of restoration of all things, which God has spoken by the mouth of all His holy prophets since the world began. [22]For Moses truly said to the fathers, The LORD your God will raise up for you a Prophet like me from your brethren. Him you shall hear in all things, whatever He says to you.

2. *Hebrews 5:5-7* So also Christ did not glorify Himself to become High Priest, but it was He who said to Him: You are My Son, today I have begotten You. [6]As He also says in another place: You are a priest forever according to the order of Melchizedek; [7]who, in the days of His flesh, when He had offered up prayers and supplications, with vehement cries and tears to Him who was able to save Him from death, and was heard because of His godly fear.

   Hebrews 7:25 Therefore He is also able to save to the uttermost those who come to God through Him, since He ever lives to make intercession for them.

3. *Psalm 2:6* Yet I have set My King on My holy hill of Zion.

   Isaiah 9:6-7 For unto us a Child is born, unto us a Son is given; and the government will be upon His shoulder. And His name will be called Wonderful, Counselor, Mighty God, Everlasting Father, Prince of Peace. [7]Of the increase of His government and peace there will be no end, upon the throne of David and over His kingdom, to order it and establish it with judgment and justice from that time forward, even forever. The zeal of the LORD of hosts will perform this.

   Matthew 21:5 Tell the daughter of Zion, Behold, your King is coming to you, lowly, and sitting on a donkey, a colt, the foal of a donkey.

25. How does Christ execute the office of a prophet?

Christ executes the office of a prophet in revealing to His people, by His word and Spirit, the will of God for their salvation.[1]

1. *John 1:18* No one has seen God at any time. The only begotten Son, who is in the bosom of the Father, He has declared Him.

   1 Peter 1:10-12 Of this salvation the prophets have inquired and searched diligently, who prophesied of the grace that would come to you, [11]searching what, or what manner of time, the Spirit of Christ who was in them was indicating when He testified beforehand the sufferings of Christ and the glories that would follow. [12]To them it was revealed that, not to themselves, but to us they were ministering the things which now have been reported to you through those who have preached the gospel to you by the Holy Spirit sent from heaven—things which angels desire to look into.

   John 20:31 But these are written that you may believe that Jesus is the Christ, the Son of God, and that believing you may have life in His name.

   John 14:26 But the Helper, the Holy Spirit, whom the Father will send in My name, He will teach you all things, and bring to your remembrance all things that I said to you.

26. How does Christ execute the office of a priest?

Christ executes the office of a priest in His once offering up of Himself a sacrifice for the sins of His people to satisfy divine justice,[1] and to reconcile them to God,[2] and in making continual intercession for them.[3]

1. *Hebrews 9:14, 28* How much more shall the blood of Christ, who through the eternal Spirit offered Himself without spot to God, purge your conscience from dead works to serve the living God? [28]So Christ was offered once to bear the sins of many. To those who eagerly wait for Him He will appear a second time, apart from sin, for salvation.

2. *Hebrews 2:17* Therefore, in all things He had to be made like His brethren, that He might be a merciful and faithful High Priest in things pertaining to God, to make propitiation for the sins of the people.

   Romans 5:10 For if when we were enemies we were reconciled to God through the death of His Son, much more, having been reconciled, we shall be saved by His life.

3. *Hebrews 7:24-25* But He, because He continues forever, has an unchangeable priesthood. [25]Therefore He is also able to save to the uttermost those who come to God through Him, since He ever lives to make intercession for them.

27. How does Christ execute the office of a king?

Christ executes the office of a king in calling His church out of the world to be a people for Himself,[1] and in ruling[2] and defending it;[3] subduing,[4] saving,[5] preserving[6] and blessing[7] His elect; and in restraining, conquering, and taking vengeance on all His and their enemies.[8]

1. *Acts 15:14-16* Simon has declared how God at the first visited the Gentiles to take out of them a people for His name. [15]And with this the words of the prophets agree, just as it is written: [16]After this I will return and will rebuild the tabernacle of David which has fallen down. I will rebuild its ruins, and I will set it up.

   Matthew 16:18 And I also say to you that you are Peter, and on this rock I will build My church, and the gates of Hades shall not prevail against it.

1 Peter 2:9-10 But you are a chosen generation, a royal priesthood, a holy nation, His own special people, that you may proclaim the praises of Him who called you out of darkness into His marvelous light; [10]who once were not a people but are now the people of God, who had not obtained mercy but now have obtained mercy.

2. *Ephesians 1:22* And He put all things under His feet, and gave Him to be head over all things to the church.

   Ephesians 4:11-12 And He Himself gave some to be apostles, some prophets, some evangelists, and some pastors and teachers, [12]for the equipping of the saints for the work of ministry, for the edifying of the body of Christ.

   Isaiah 33:22 For the LORD is our Judge, the LORD is our Lawgiver, the LORD is our King; He will save us.

3. *Matthew 16:18* And I also say to you that you are Peter, and on this rock I will build My church, and the gates of Hades shall not prevail against it.

   Isaiah 32:1-2 Behold, a king will reign in righteousness, and princes will rule with justice. [2]A man will be as a hiding place from the wind, and a cover from the tempest, as rivers of water in a dry place, as the shadow of a great rock in a weary land.

   Isaiah 33:22 For the LORD is our Judge, the LORD is our Lawgiver, the LORD is our King; He will save us.

4. *Psalm 110:2-3* The LORD shall send the rod of Your strength out of Zion. Rule in the midst of Your enemies! [3]Your people shall be volunteers in the day of Your power; in the beauties of holiness, from the womb of the morning, You have the dew of Your youth.

5. *Acts 5:31* Him God has exalted to His right hand to be Prince and Savior, to give repentance to Israel and forgiveness of sins.

6. *Isaiah 63:9* In all their affliction He was afflicted, and the Angel of His Presence saved them; in His love and in His pity He redeemed them; and He bore them and carried them all the days of old.

7. *Revelation 2:10* Do not fear any of those things which you are about to suffer. Indeed, the devil is about to throw some of you into prison, that you may be tested, and you will have tribulation ten days. Be faithful until death, and I will give you the crown of life.

   Revelation 22:12 And behold, I am coming quickly, and My reward is with Me, to give to each one according to his work.

8. *1 Corinthians 15:25* For He must reign till He has put all enemies under His feet.

   2 Thessalonians 1:8-9 In flaming fire taking vengeance on those who do not know God, and on those who do not obey the gospel of our Lord Jesus Christ. [9]These shall be punished with everlasting destruction from the presence of the Lord and from the glory of His power.

28. Wherein did Christ's humiliation consist?

Christ's humiliation consisted in His being born,[1] and that in a low condition,[1] made under the law,[2] undergoing the miseries of this life,[3] the wrath of God,[4] and the cursed death of the cross;[5] in being buried[6] and continuing under the power of death for a time.[7]

1. *Luke 2:7* And she brought forth her firstborn Son, and wrapped Him in swaddling cloths, and laid Him in a manger, because there was no room for them in the inn.

2. *Galatians 4:4* But when the fullness of the time had come, God sent forth His Son, born of a woman, born under the law.

3. *Hebrews 12:2-3* Looking unto Jesus, the author and finisher of our faith, who for the joy that was set before Him endured the cross, despising the shame, and has sat down at the

right hand of the throne of God. ³For consider Him who endured such hostility from sinners against Himself, lest you become weary and discouraged in your souls.

Isaiah 53:2-3 For He shall grow up before Him as a tender plant, and as a root out of dry ground. He has no form or comeliness; and when we see Him, there is no beauty that we should desire Him. ³He is despised and rejected by men, a man of sorrows and acquainted with grief. And we hid, as it were, our faces from Him; He was despised, and we did not esteem Him.

4. *Luke 22:44* And being in agony, He prayed more earnestly. And His sweat became like great drops of blood falling down to the ground.

Matthew 27:46 And about the ninth hour Jesus cried out with a loud voice, saying, Eli, Eli, lama sabachthani? that is, My God, My God, why have You forsaken Me?

5. *Philippians 2:8* And being found in appearance as a man, He humbled Himself and became obedient to the point of death, even the death of the cross.

6. *1 Corinthians 15:3-4* For I delivered to you first of all that which I also received: that Christ died for our sins according to the Scriptures, ⁴and that He was buried, and that He rose again the third day according to the Scriptures.

7. *Acts 2:24-27, 31* Whom God raised up, having loosed the pains of death, because it was not possible that He should be held by it. ²⁵For David says concerning Him: I foresaw the Lord always before my face, for He is at my right hand, that I may not be shaken; ²⁶therefore my heart rejoiced, and my tongue was glad; moreover my flesh will also rest in hope, ²⁷because You will not leave my soul in Hades, nor will You allow Your Holy One to see corruption. ³¹He, foreseeing this, spoke concerning the resurrection of the Christ, that His soul was not left in Hades, nor did His flesh see corruption.

29. Wherein consists Christ's exaltation?

Christ's exaltation consists in His rising again from the dead on the third day,¹ in ascending up into heaven,² in sitting at the right hand of God the Father,³ and in coming to judge the world at the last day.⁴

1. *1 Corinthians 15:4* And that He was buried, and that He rose again the third day according to the Scriptures.

2. *Mark 16:19* So then, after the Lord had spoken to them, He was received up into heaven, and sat down at the right hand of God.

Acts 1:9-11 Now when He had spoken these things, while they watched, He was taken up, and a cloud received Him out of their sight. ¹⁰And while they looked steadfastly toward heaven as He went up, behold, two men stood by them in white apparel, ¹¹who also said, Men of Galilee, why do you stand gazing up into heaven? This same Jesus, who was taken up from you into heaven, will so come in like manner as you saw Him go into heaven.

3. *Ephesians 1:20-21* Which He worked in Christ when He raised Him from the dead and seated Him at His right hand in the heavenly places, ²¹far above all principality and power and might and dominion, and every name that is named, not only in this age but also in that which is to come.

4. *Acts 17:31* Because He has appointed a day on which He will judge the world in righteousness by the Man whom He has ordained. He has given assurance of this to all by raising Him from the dead.

30. How are God's elect made partakers of the redemption purchased by Christ?

God's elect are made partakers of the redemption purchased by Christ, by God the Father's[1] effectual application of it to them[2] by His Holy Spirit.[3]

1. *Romans 8:29* For whom He foreknew, He also predestined to be conformed to the image of His Son, that He might be the firstborn among many brethren.

2. *John 1:11-12* He came to His own, and His own did not receive Him. [12]But as many as received Him, to them He gave the right to become children of God, even to those who believe in His name.

3. *Titus 3:5-6* Not by works of righteousness which we have done, but according to His mercy He saved us, through the washing of regeneration and renewing of the Holy Spirit, [6]whom He poured out on us abundantly through Jesus Christ our Savior.

31. How does the Father by the Spirit apply to His elect the redemption purchased by Christ?

The Father by the Spirit applies to His elect the redemption purchased by Christ, by working faith in them,[1] and uniting them to Christ in their effectual calling.[2]

1. *John 6:37, 39* All that the Father gives Me will come to Me, and the one who comes to Me I will by no means cast out. [39]This is the will of the Father who sent Me, that of all He has given Me I should lose nothing, but should raise it up at the last day.

   Ephesians 2:8 For by grace you have been saved through faith, and that not of yourselves; it is the gift of God.

   Philippians 1:29 For to you it has been granted on behalf of Christ, not only to believe in Him, but also to suffer for His sake.

   John 1:12-13 But as many as received Him, to them He gave the right to become children of God, even to those who believe in His name: [13]who were born, not of blood, nor of the will of the flesh, nor of the will of man, but of God. *Compared with John 3:5* Jesus answered, Most assuredly, I say to you, unless one is born of water and the Spirit, he cannot enter the kingdom of God.

2. *1 Corinthians 1:9* God is faithful, by whom you were called into the fellowship of His Son, Jesus Christ our Lord.

   John 6:44 No one can come to Me unless the Father who sent Me draws him; and I will raise him up at the last day.

32. What is effectual calling?

Effectual calling is the work of God the Father's power and grace,[1] whereby He,[2] by His word[3] and Spirit,[4] invites and draws[5] His elect[6] unto Jesus Christ; convincing them of their sin and misery,[7] enlightening their minds in the knowledge of Christ,[8] and renewing their wills,[9] thereby persuading and enabling them to embrace Jesus Christ, freely offered to all in the gospel.[10]

1. *2 Timothy 1:8-9* Therefore do not be ashamed of the testimony of our Lord, nor of me His prisoner, but share with me in the sufferings for the gospel according to the power

of God, [9]who has saved us and called us with a holy calling, not according to our works, but according to His own purpose and grace which was given to us in Christ Jesus before time began.

2. *1 Corinthians 1:9* God is faithful, by whom you were called into the fellowship of His Son, Jesus Christ our Lord.

   Romans 8:29-30 For whom He foreknew, He also predestined to be conformed to the image of His Son, that He might be the firstborn among many brethren. [30]Moreover whom He predestined, these He also called; whom He called, these He also justified; and whom He justified, these He also glorified.

3. *2 Thessalonians 2:13-14* But we are bound to give thanks to God always for you, brethren beloved by the Lord, because God from the beginning chose you for salvation through sanctification by the Spirit and belief in the truth, [14]to which He called you by our gospel, for the obtaining of the glory of our Lord Jesus Christ.

   James 1:18 Of His own will He brought us forth by the word of truth, that we might be a kind of firstfruits of His creatures.

   1 Peter 1:23, 25 Having been born again, not of corruptible seed but incorruptible, through the word of God which lives and abides forever, [25]but the word of the Lord endures forever. Now this is the word which by the gospel was preached to you.

4. *John 6:63* It is the Spirit who gives life; the flesh profits nothing. The words that I speak to you are spirit, and they are life.

   John 1:12-13 But as many as received Him, to them He gave the right to become children of God, even to those who believe in His name: [13]who were born, not of blood, nor of the will of the flesh, nor of the will of man, but of God. *Compared with John 3:5* Jesus answered, Most assuredly, I say to you, unless one is born of water and the Spirit, he cannot enter the kingdom of God.

5. *1 Corinthians 1:9* God is faithful, by whom you were called into the fellowship of His Son, Jesus Christ our Lord.

   John 6:44 No one can come to Me unless the Father who sent Me draws him; and I will raise him up at the last day.

6. *Romans 8:29-30* For whom He foreknew, He also predestined to be conformed to the image of His Son, that He might be the firstborn among many brethren. [30]Moreover whom He predestined, these He also called; whom He called, these He also justified; and whom He justified, these He also glorified.

7. *John 16:8-11* And when He has come, He will convict the world of sin, and of righteousness, and of judgment: [9]of sin, because they do not believe in Me; [10]of righteousness, because I go to My Father and you see Me no more; [11]of judgment, because the ruler of this world is judged.

8. *Matthew 16:16-17* And Simon Peter answered and said, You are the Christ, the Son of the living God. [17]Jesus answered and said to him, Blessed are you, Simon Bar-Jonah, for flesh and blood has not revealed this to you, but My Father who is in heaven.

   Acts 26:18 To open their eyes and to turn them from darkness to light, and from the power of Satan to God, that they may receive forgiveness of sins and an inheritance among those who are sanctified by faith in Me.

9. *Ezekiel 36:26-27* I will give you a new heart and put a new spirit within you; I will take the heart of stone out of your flesh and give you a heart of flesh. [27]I will put My Spirit within you and cause you to walk in My statutes, and you will keep My judgments and do them.

   Psalm 110:3 Your people shall be volunteers in the day of Your power; in the beauties of holiness, from the womb of the morning, You have the dew of Your youth.

10. *John 6:44-45* No one can come to Me unless the Father who sent Me draws him; and I will raise him up at the last day. [45]It is written in the prophets, And they shall all be

taught by God. Therefore everyone who has heard and learned from the Father comes to Me.

Philippians 2:13 For it is God who works in you both to will and to do for His good pleasure.

Deuteronomy 30:6 And the LORD your God will circumcise your heart and the heart of your descendants, to love the LORD your God with all your heart and with all your soul, that you may live.

Matthew 11:25-28 At that time Jesus answered and said, I thank You, Father, Lord of heaven and earth, because You have hidden these things from the wise and prudent and have revealed them to babes. [26]Even so, Father, for so it seemed good in Your sight. [27]All things have been delivered to Me by My Father, and no one knows the Son except the Father. Nor does anyone know the Father except the Son, and he to whom the Son wills to reveal Him. [28]Come to Me, all you who labor and are heavy laden, and I will give you rest.

33. What benefits do they that are effectually called partake of in this life?

They that are effectually called do in this life partake of justification,[1] adoption,[2] and sanctification, and the several benefits which in this life, do either accompany or flow from them.[3]

1. *Romans 8:30* Moreover whom He predestined, these He also called; whom He called, these He also justified; and whom He justified, these He also glorified.
2. *Ephesians 1:5* Having predestined us to adoption as sons by Jesus Christ to Himself, according to the good pleasure of His will.
3. *1 Corinthians 6:11* And such were some of you. But you were washed, but you were sanctified, but you were justified in the name of the Lord Jesus and by the Spirit of our God.

   1 Corinthians 1:26, 30 For you see your calling, brethren, that not many wise according to the flesh, not many mighty, not many noble, are called. [30]But of Him you are in Christ Jesus, who became for us wisdom from God—and righteousness and sanctification and redemption.

34. What is justification?

Justification is an act of God's free grace[1] unto sinners effectually called to Jesus Christ,[2] wherein He pardons all their sins,[3] and accepts them as righteous in His sight,[4] only for the righteousness of Christ imputed to them,[5] and received by faith alone.[6]

1. *Romans 3:24-25* Being justified freely by His grace through the redemption that is in Christ Jesus, [25]whom God set forth to be a propitiation by His blood, through faith, to demonstrate His righteousness, because in His forbearance God had passed over the sins that were previously committed.
2. *Romans 8:30* Moreover whom He predestined, these He also called; whom He called, these He also justified; and whom He justified, these He also glorified.
3. *Romans 4:6-8* Just as David also describes the blessedness of the man to whom God imputes righteousness apart from works: [7]blessed are those whose lawless deeds are forgiven, and whose sins are covered; [8]blessed is the man to whom the Lord shall not impute sin.

17

4. *2 Corinthians 5:19, 21* That is, that God was in Christ reconciling the world to Himself, not imputing their trespasses to them, and has committed to us the word of reconciliation. [21]For He made Him who knew no sin to be sin for us, that we might become the righteousness of God in Him.

5. *Romans 5:17-19* For if by the one man's offense death reigned through the one, much more those who receive abundance of grace and of the gift of righteousness will reign in life through the One, Jesus Christ. [18]Therefore, as through one man's offense judgment came to all men, resulting in condemnation, even so through one Man's righteous act the free gift came to all men, resulting in justification of life. [19]For as by one man's disobedience many were made sinners, so also by one Man's obedience many will be made righteous.

6. *Galatians 2:16* Knowing that a man is not justified by the works of the law but by faith in Jesus Christ, even we have believed in Christ Jesus, that we might be justified by faith in Christ and not by the works of the law; for by the works of the law no flesh shall be justified.

   Philippians 3:9 And be found in Him, not having my own righteousness, which is from the law, but that which is through faith in Christ, the righteousness which is from God by faith.

35. What is adoption?

Adoption is an act of God's free grace,[1] whereby all those who are justified are received into the number, and have a right to all the privileges of the sons of God.[2]

1. *1 John 3:1* Behold what manner of love the Father has bestowed on us, that we should be called children of God! Therefore the world does not know us, because it did not know Him.

2. *John 1:12* But as many as received Him, to them He gave the right to become children of God, even to those who believe in His name.

   Romans 8:17 And if children, then heirs—heirs of God and joint heirs with Christ, if indeed we suffer with Him, that we may also be glorified together.

36. What is sanctification?

Sanctification is the work of God's free grace,[1] whereby His elect are renewed in the whole man after the image of God,[2] and are enabled more and more to die unto sin, and live unto righteousness.[3]

1. *2 Thessalonians 2:13* But we are bound to give thanks to God always for you, brethren beloved by the Lord, because God from the beginning chose you for salvation through sanctification by the Spirit and belief in the truth.

2. *Ephesians 4:23-24* And be renewed in the spirit of your mind, [24]and that you put on the new man which was created according to God, in righteousness and true holiness.

   Romans 6:4-6 Therefore we were buried with Him through baptism into death, that just as Christ was raised from the dead by the glory of the Father, even so we also should walk in newness of life. [5]For if we have been united together in the likeness of His death, certainly we also shall be in the likeness of His resurrection, [6]knowing this, that our old man was crucified with Him, that the body of sin might be done away with, that we should no longer be slaves of sin.

   Galatians 5:24 And those who are Christ's have crucified the flesh with its passions and desires.

3. *1 John 5:4* For whatever is born of God overcomes the world. And this is the victory that has overcome the world—our faith.

Romans 8:1 There is therefore now no condemnation to those who are in Christ Jesus, who do not walk according to the flesh, but according to the Spirit.

Philippians 1:6 Being confident of this very thing, that He who has begun a good work in you will complete it until the day of Jesus Christ.

Philippians 2:12-13 Therefore, my beloved, as you have always obeyed, not as in my presence only, but now much more in my absence, work out your own salvation with fear and trembling; [13]for it is God who works in you both to will and to do for His good pleasure.

37. What are the benefits which in this life do accompany or flow from justification, adoption, and sanctification?

The benefits which in this life do accompany or flow from justification, adoption, and sanctification, are assurance of God's love, peace of conscience,[1] joy in the Holy Spirit,[2] increase of grace,[3] and perseverance therein to the end.[4]

1. *Romans 5:1-2, 5* Therefore, having been justified by faith, we have peace with God through our Lord Jesus Christ, [2]through whom also we have access by faith into this grace in which we stand, and rejoice in hope of the glory of God. [5]Now hope does not disappoint, because the love of God has been poured out in our hearts by the Holy Spirit who was given to us.

2. *Romans 14:17* For the kingdom of God is not food and drink, but righteousness and peace and joy in the Holy Spirit.

3. *Proverbs 4:18* But the path of the just is like the shining sun, that shines ever brighter unto the perfect day.

4. *1 Peter 1:5* Who are kept by the power of God through faith for salvation ready to be revealed in the last time.

38. What benefits do believers receive from Christ at death?

The souls of believers are, at their death, made perfect in holiness,[1] and do immediately pass into glory;[2] and their bodies, being still united to Christ,[3] do rest in their graves[4] until the resurrection.[5]

1. *Hebrews 12:23* To the general assembly and church of the firstborn who are registered in heaven, to God the Judge of all, to the spirits of just men made perfect.

2. *2 Corinthians 5:1, 6, 8* For we know that if our earthly house, this tent, is destroyed, we have a building from God, a house not made with hands, eternal in the heavens. [6]Therefore we are always confident, knowing that while we are at home in the body we are absent from the Lord. [8]We are confident, yes, well pleased rather to be absent from the body and to be present with the Lord.

Philippians 1:23 For I am hard pressed between the two, having a desire to depart and be with Christ, which is far better.

Luke 23:43 And Jesus said to him, Assuredly, I say to you, today you will be with Me in Paradise.

3. *1 Thessalonians 4:14* For if we believe that Jesus died and rose again, even so God will bring with Him those who sleep in Jesus.

4. *Isaiah 57:2* He shall enter into peace; they shall rest in their beds, each one walking in his uprightness.

5. *Job 19:26-27* And after my skin is destroyed, this I know, that in my flesh I shall see God, [27]whom I shall see for myself, and my eyes shall behold, and not another. How my heart yearns within me!

1 Thessalonians 4:16 For the Lord Himself will descend from heaven with a shout, with the voice of an archangel, and with the trumpet of God. And the dead in Christ will rise first.

39. What shall be done to the wicked at their death?

The souls of the wicked are, at their death, cast into the torments of hell, and their bodies lie in their graves[1] until the resurrection and judgment of the great day.[2]

1. *Luke 16:23-24* And being in torments in Hades, he lifted up his eyes and saw Abraham afar off, and Lazarus in his bosom. [24]Then he cried and said, Father Abraham, have mercy on me, and send Lazarus that he may dip the tip of his finger in water and cool my tongue; for I am tormented in this flame.

2. *Acts 24:15* I have hope in God, which they themselves also accept, that there will be a resurrection of the dead, both of the just and the unjust.

   John 5:28-29 Do not marvel at this; for the hour is coming in which all who are in the graves will hear His voice [29]and come forth—those who have done good, to the resurrection of life, and those who have done evil, to the resurrection of condemnation.

   2 Peter 2:9 Then the Lord knows how to deliver the godly out of temptations and to reserve the unjust under punishment for the day of judgment.

40. What benefits do believers receive from Christ at the resurrection?

At the resurrection, believers being raised up in glory,[1] shall be openly acknowledged and acquitted in the day of judgment,[2] and made perfectly blessed in the full enjoyment of God[3] to all eternity.[4]

1. *Philippians 3:21* Who will transform our lowly body that it may be conformed to His glorious body, according to the working by which He is able even to subdue all things to Himself.

   1 Corinthians 15:42-43 So also is the resurrection of the dead. The body is sown in corruption, it is raised in incorruption. [43]It is sown in dishonor, it is raised in glory. It is sown in weakness, it is raised in power.

2. *Matthew 25:23* His lord said to him, Well done, good and faithful servant; you have been faithful over a few things, I will make you ruler over many things. Enter into the joy of your lord.

   Matthew 10:32 Therefore whoever confesses Me before men, him I will also confess before My Father who is in heaven.

3. *1 John 3:2* Beloved, now we are children of God; and it has not yet been revealed what we shall be, but we know that when He is revealed, we shall be like Him, for we shall see Him as He is.

   1 Corinthians 13:12 For now we see in a mirror, dimly, but then face to face. Now I know in part, but then I shall know just as I also am known.

4. *1 Thessalonians 4:17-18* Then we who are alive and remain shall be caught up together with them in the clouds to meet the Lord in the air. And thus we shall always be with the Lord. [18]Therefore comfort one another with these words.

41. What shall be done to the wicked at the day of judgment?

At the day of judgment,[1] the wicked being raised to dishonor,[2] shall be sentenced to the unspeakable torments of body and soul in hell[3] with the devil and his angels for all eternity.[4]

1. *John 5:28-29* Do not marvel at this; for the hour is coming in which all who are in the graves will hear His voice [29]and come forth—those who have done good, to the resurrection of life, and those who have done evil, to the resurrection of condemnation.
2. *Daniel 12:2* And many of those who sleep in the dust of the earth shall awake, some to everlasting life, some to shame and everlasting contempt.
3. *2 Thessalonians 1:8-9* In flaming fire taking vengeance on those who do not know God, and on those who do not obey the gospel of our Lord Jesus Christ. [9]These shall be punished with everlasting destruction from the presence of the Lord and from the glory of His power.
   Matthew 13:49-50 So it will be at the end of the age. The angels will come forth, separate the wicked from among the just, [50]and cast them into the furnace of fire. There will be wailing and gnashing of teeth.
   Revelation 14:10-11 He himself shall also drink of the wine of the wrath of God, which is poured out full strength into the cup of His indignation. And he shall be tormented with fire and brimstone in the presence of the holy angels and in the presence of the Lamb. [11]And the smoke of their torment ascends forever and ever; and they have no rest day or night, who worship the beast and his image, and whoever receives the mark of his name.
4. *Matthew 25:41, 46* Then He will also say to those on the left hand, Depart from Me, you cursed, into the everlasting fire prepared for the devil and his angels. [46]And these will go away into everlasting punishment, but the righteous into eternal life.

42. What is the duty which God requires of man?

The duty which God requires of man is obedience to His revealed will.[1]

1. *Ecclesiastes 12:13-14* Let us hear the conclusion of the whole matter: Fear God and keep His commandments, for this is the whole duty of man. [14]For God will bring every work into judgment, including every secret thing, whether it is good or whether it is evil.
   Micah 6:8 He has shown you, O man, what is good; and what does the LORD require of you but to do justly, to love mercy, and to walk humbly with your God?

43. What did God at first reveal to man for the rule of his obedience?

The rule which God at first revealed to man for his obedience was the moral law.[1]

1. *Romans 2:14-15* For when Gentiles, who do not have the law, by nature do the things contained in the law, these, although not having the law, are a law to themselves, [15]who show the work of the law written in their hearts, their conscience also bearing witness, and between themselves their thoughts accusing or else excusing them.

44. Where is the moral law summarily comprehended?

The moral law is summarily comprehended in the ten commandments.[1]

1. *Deuteronomy 10:4* And He wrote on the tablets according to the first writing, the Ten Commandments, which the LORD had spoken to you in the mountain from the midst of the fire in the day of the assembly; and the LORD gave them to me.

Matthew 19:17 So He said to him, Why do you call Me good? No one is good but One, that is, God. But if you want to enter into life, keep the commandments.

45. What is the sum of the ten commandments?

The sum of the ten commandments is, to love the Lord our God with all our heart, with all our soul, with all our strength, and with all our mind; and our neighbor as ourselves.[1]

1. *Matthew 22:37-40* Jesus said to him, You shall love the Lord your God with all your heart, with all your soul, and with all your mind. [38]This is the first and great commandment. [39]And the second is like it: You shall love your neighbor as yourself. [40]On these two commandments hang all the Law and the Prophets.

46. What is the preface to the ten commandments?

The preface to the ten commandments is in these words, I am the LORD your God, who brought you out of the land of Egypt, out of the house of bondage.[1]

1. *Exodus 20:2*

47. What does the preface to the ten commandments teach us?

The preface to the ten commandments teaches us that because God is the LORD, and our God, and the Redeemer, therefore we are bound to keep all His commandments.[1]

1. *Psalm 100:2-3* Serve the LORD with gladness; come before His presence with singing. [3]Know that the LORD, He is God; it is He who has made us, and not we ourselves; we are His people and the sheep of His pasture.

Jeremiah 10:7 Who would not fear You, O King of the nations? For this is Your rightful due, for among all the wise men of the nations, and in all their kingdoms, there is none like You.

Deuteronomy 11:1 Therefore you shall love the LORD your God, and keep His charge, His statutes, His judgments, and His commandments always.

Luke 1:74-75 To grant us that we, being delivered from the hand of our enemies, might serve Him without fear, [75]in holiness and righteousness before Him all the days of our life.

48. What is the first commandment?

The first commandment is, You shall have no other gods before Me.[1]

1. *Exodus 20:3*

49. What is required in the first commandment?

The first commandment requires us to know and acknowledge God to be the only true God, and our God;[1] and to worship and glorify Him accordingly.[2]

1. *1 Chronicles 28:9* As for you, my son Solomon, know the God of your father, and serve Him with a loyal heart and with a willing mind; for the LORD searches all hearts and understands all the intent of the thoughts. If you seek Him, He will be found by you; but if you forsake Him, He will cast you off forever.

   Deuteronomy 26:17 Today you have proclaimed the LORD to be your God, and that you will walk in His ways and keep His statutes, His commandments, and His judgments, and that you will obey His voice.

2. *Matthew 4:10* Then Jesus said to him, Away with you, Satan! For it is written, You shall worship the LORD your God, and Him only you shall serve.

   Psalm 29:2 Give unto the LORD the glory due to His name; worship the LORD in the beauty of holiness.

50. What is forbidden in the first commandment?

The first commandment forbids the denying,[1] or not worshipping and glorifying the true God as God,[2] and our God;[3] and the giving of that worship and glory to any other which is due to Him alone.[4]

1. *Psalm 14:1* The fool has said in his heart, There is no God. They are corrupt, they have done abominable works, there is none who does good.

2. *Romans 1:20-21* For since the creation of the world His invisible attributes are clearly seen, being understood by the things that are made, even His eternal power and Godhead, so that they are without excuse, [21]because, although they knew God, they did not glorify Him as God, nor were thankful, but became futile in their thoughts, and their foolish hearts were darkened.

3. *Psalm 81:10-11* I am the LORD your God, who brought you out of the land of Egypt; open your mouth wide, and I will fill it. [11]But My people would not heed My voice, and Israel would have none of Me.

4. *Romans 1:25-26* Who exchanged the truth of God for the lie, and worshiped and served the creature rather than the Creator, who is blessed forever. Amen. [26]For this reason God gave them up to vile passions. For even their women exchanged the natural use for what is against nature.

51. What are we specially taught by the words "before Me" in the first commandment?

The words "before Me" in the first commandment teach us that God—who sees all things—takes notice of, and is much displeased with, the sin of having any other god.[1]

1. *Psalm 44:20-21* If we had forgotten the name of our God, or stretched out our hands to a foreign god, [21]would not God search this out? For He knows the secrets of the heart.

52. What is the second commandment?

The second commandment is, You shall not make for yourself any carved image, or any likeness of anything that is in heaven above, or that is in the earth beneath, or that is in the water under the earth; you shall not bow down to them nor serve them. For I, the LORD your God, am a jealous God, visiting the iniquity of the fathers on the children to the third and fourth generations of those who hate Me, but showing mercy to thousands, to those who love Me and keep My commandments.[1]

1. *Exodus 20:4-6*

53. What is required in the second commandment?

The second commandment requires the receiving, observing,[1] and keeping pure and entire, all such religious worship and ordinances as God has appointed in His word.[2]

1. *John 4:24* God is Spirit, and those who worship Him must worship in spirit and truth.
Deuteronomy 32:46 And He said to them: Set your hearts on all the words which I testify among you today, which you shall command your children to be careful to observe—all the words of this law.
Matthew 28:20 Teaching them to observe all things that I have commanded you; and lo, I am with you always, even to the end of the age. Amen.
Acts 2:42 And they continued steadfastly in the apostles' doctrine and fellowship, in the breaking of bread, and in prayers.
2. *Deuteronomy 12:13-14* Take heed to yourself that you do not offer your burnt offerings in every place that you see; [14]but in the place which the LORD chooses, in one of your tribes, there you shall offer your burnt offerings, and there you shall do all that I command you.
Deuteronomy 12:32 Whatever I command you, be careful to observe it; you shall not add to it nor take away from it.
Mark 7:6-8 He answered and said to them, Well did Isaiah prophesy of you hypocrites, as it is written: This people honors Me with their lips, but their heart is far from Me. [7]And in vain they worship Me, teaching as doctrines the commandments of men. [8]For laying aside the commandment of God, you hold the tradition of men.

54. What is forbidden in the second commandment?

The second commandment forbids the worshipping of God by images,[1] or any other way not appointed in His word.[2]

1. *Deuteronomy 4:15-19* Take careful heed to yourselves, for you saw no form when the LORD spoke to you at Horeb out of the midst of the fire, [16]lest you act corruptly and make for yourselves a carved image in the form of any figure: the likeness of male or female, [17]the likeness of any beast that is on the earth or the likeness of any winged bird that flies in the air, [18]the likeness of anything that creeps on the ground or the likeness of any fish that is in the water beneath the earth. [19]And take heed, lest you lift your eyes to heaven, and when you see the sun, the moon, and the stars, all the host of heaven, you feel driven to worship them and serve them, which the LORD your God has given to all the peoples under the whole heaven as a heritage.

2. *Leviticus 10:1-2* Then Nadab and Abihu, the sons of Aaron, each took his censer and put fire in it, put incense on it, and offered profane fire before the LORD, which He had not commanded them. ²So fire went out from the LORD and devoured them, and they died before the LORD.

Deuteronomy 12:30-32 Take heed to yourself that you are not ensnared to follow them, after they are destroyed from before you, and that you do not inquire after their gods, saying, How did these nations serve their gods? I also will do likewise. ³¹You shall not worship the LORD your God in that way; for every abomination to the LORD which He hates they have done to their gods; for they burn even their sons and daughters in the fire to their gods. ³²Whatever I command you, be careful to observe it; you shall not add to it nor take away from it.

55. What are the reasons annexed to the second commandment?

The reasons annexed to the second commandment are, God's sovereignty over us, His ownership of us,[1] and the zeal He has to His own worship.[2]

1. *Psalm 95:2-3, 6* Let us come before His presence with thanksgiving; Let us shout joyfully to Him with psalms. ³For the LORD is the great God, and the great King above all gods. ⁶Oh come, let us worship and bow down; let us kneel before the LORD our Maker. For He is our God, and we are the people of His pasture, and the sheep of His hand.

   Psalm 100:2-3 Serve the LORD with gladness; come before His presence with singing. ³Know that the LORD, He is God; it is He who has made us, and not we ourselves; we are His people and the sheep of His pasture.

2. *Exodus 34:13-14* But you shall destroy their altars, break their sacred pillars, and cut down their wooden images ¹⁴(for you shall worship no other god, for the LORD, whose name is Jealous, is a jealous God).

   Psalm 106:19, 21, 23 They made a calf in Horeb, and worshiped the molded image. ²¹They forgot God their Savior, who had done great things in Egypt, ²³therefore He said that He would destroy them, had not Moses His chosen one stood before Him in the breach, to turn away His wrath, lest He destroy them.

56. What is the third commandment?

The third commandment is, You shall not take the name of the LORD your God in vain, for the LORD will not hold him guiltless who takes His name in vain.[1]

1. *Exodus 20:7*

57. What is required in the third commandment?

The third commandment requires the holy and reverent use of God's names, titles,[1] attributes,[2] ordinances,[3] word,[4] and works.[5]

1. *Matthew 6:9* In this manner, therefore, pray: Our Father in heaven, hallowed be Your name.

   Psalm 29:2 Give unto the LORD the glory due to His name; worship the LORD in the beauty of holiness.

2. *Revelation 15:3-4* And they sing the song of Moses, the servant of God, and the song of the Lamb, saying: Great and marvelous are Your works, Lord God Almighty! Just and

true are Your ways, O King of the saints! [4]Who shall not fear You, O Lord, and glorify Your name? For You alone are holy. For all nations shall come and worship before You, for Your judgments have been manifested.

3. *Malachi 1:11, 14* For from the rising of the sun, even to its going down, My name shall be great among the Gentiles; In every place incense shall be offered to My name, and a pure offering; For My name shall be great among the nations, says the LORD of hosts. [14]But cursed be the deceiver who has in his flock a male, and makes a vow, but sacrifices to the Lord what is blemished—for I am a great King, says the LORD of hosts, and My name is to be feared among the nations.

   Ecclesiastes 5:1 Walk prudently when you go to the house of God; and draw near to hear rather than to give the sacrifice of fools, for they do not know that they do evil.

4. *Psalm 138:1-2* I will praise You with my whole heart; before the gods I will sing praises to You. [2]I will worship toward Your holy temple, and praise Your name for Your lovingkindness and Your truth; for You have magnified Your word above all Your name.

5. *Psalm 105:1-5* Oh, give thanks to the LORD! Call upon His name; Make known His deeds among the peoples. [2]Sing to Him, sing psalms to Him; talk of all His wondrous works. [3]Glory in His holy name; let the hearts of those rejoice who seek the LORD. [4]Seek the LORD and His strength; Seek His face evermore. [5]Remember His marvelous works which He has done, His wonders, and the judgments of His mouth.

58. What is forbidden in the third commandment?

The third commandment forbids all profaning or abusing of any thing whereby God makes Himself known.[1]

1. *Malachi 1:6-7, 12* A son honors his father, and a servant his master. If then I am the Father, where is My honor? And if I am a Master, where is My reverence? Says the LORD of hosts to you priests who despise My name. Yet you say, In what way have we despised Your name? [7]You offer defiled food on My altar. But you say, In what way have we defiled You? By saying, The table of the LORD is contemptible. [12]But you profane it, in that you say, The table of the LORD is defiled; and its fruit, its food, is contemptible.

   Malachi 2:2 If you will not hear, and if you will not take it to heart, to give glory to My name, says the LORD of hosts, I will send a curse upon you, and I will curse your blessings. Yes, I have cursed them already, because you do not take it to heart.

   Malachi 3:14 You have said, It is vain to serve God; what profit is it that we have kept His ordinance, and that we have walked as mourners before the LORD of hosts?

59. What is the reason annexed to the third commandment?

The reason annexed to the third commandment is, that however the breakers of this commandment may escape punishment from men, yet the Lord our God will not permit them to escape His righteous judgment.[1]

1. *1 Samuel 2:12, 17, 22, 29* Now the sons of Eli were corrupt; they did not know the LORD. [17]Therefore the sin of the young men was very great before the LORD, for men abhorred the offering of the LORD. [22]Now Eli was very old; and he heard everything his sons did to all Israel, and how they lay with the women who assembled at the door of the tabernacle of meeting. [29]Why do you kick at My sacrifice and My offering which I have commanded in My habitation, and honor your sons more than Me, to make yourselves fat with the best of all the offerings of Israel My people?

   1 Samuel 3:13 For I have told him that I will judge his house forever for the iniquity which he knows, because his sons made themselves vile, and he did not restrain them.

Deuteronomy 28:58-59 If you do not carefully observe all the words of this law that are written in this book, that you may fear this glorious and awesome name, THE LORD YOUR GOD, [59]then the LORD will bring upon you and your descendants extraordinary plagues—great and prolonged plagues—and serious and prolonged sicknesses.

Malachi 2:2 If you will not hear, and if you will not take it to heart, to give glory to My name, says the LORD of hosts, I will send a curse upon you, and I will curse your blessings. Yes, I have cursed them already, because you do not take it to heart.

60. What is the fourth commandment?

The fourth commandment is, Remember the Sabbath day, to keep it holy. Six days you shall labor and do all your work, but the seventh day is the Sabbath of the LORD your God. In it you shall do no work: you, nor your son, nor your daughter, nor your manservant, nor your maidservant, nor your cattle, nor your stranger who is within your gates. For in six days the LORD made the heavens and the earth, the sea, and all that is in them, and rested the seventh day. Therefore the LORD blessed the Sabbath day and hallowed it.[1]

1. *Exodus 20:8-11*

61. What is required in the fourth commandment?

The fourth commandment requires the keeping holy to God such set times as He has appointed in His word; expressly one whole day in seven is to be a holy sabbath to Himself.[1]

1. *Leviticus 19:30* You shall keep My Sabbaths and reverence My sanctuary: I am the LORD.

Deuteronomy 5:12-14 Observe the Sabbath day, to keep it holy, as the LORD your God commanded you. [13]Six days you shall labor and do all your work, [14]but the seventh day is the Sabbath of the LORD your God. In it you shall not do any work: you, nor your son, nor your daughter, nor your manservant, nor your maidservant, nor your ox, nor your donkey, nor any of your cattle, nor your stranger who is within your gates, that your manservant and your maidservant may rest as well as you.

62. Which day of the seven has God appointed to be the weekly Sabbath?

From the beginning of the world to the resurrection of Christ, God appointed the seventh day of the week to be the weekly Sabbath;[1] and the first day of the week ever since, to continue to the end of the world, which is the Christian Sabbath.[2]

1. *Genesis 2:2-3* And on the seventh day God ended His work which He had done, and He rested on the seventh day from all His work which He had done. [3]Then God blessed the seventh day and sanctified it, because in it He rested from all His work which God had created and made.

2. *1 Corinthians 16:1-2* Now concerning the collection for the saints, as I have given orders to the churches of Galatia, so you must do also: [2]On the first day of the week let

each one of you lay something aside, storing up as he may prosper, that there be no collections when I come.

Acts 20:7 Now on the first day of the week, when the disciples came together to break bread, Paul, ready to depart the next day, spoke to them and continued his message until midnight.

Revelation 1:10 I was in the Spirit on the Lord's Day, and I heard behind me a loud voice, as of a trumpet.

63. How is the Sabbath to be sanctified?

The Sabbath is to be sanctified by a holy resting all that day,[1] even from such worldly employments and recreations as are lawful on the other days;[2] and spending the whole time in the public and private exercises of God's worship,[3] except so much as is to be taken up in the works of necessity and mercy.[4]

1. *Leviticus 23:3* Six days shall work be done, but the seventh day is a Sabbath of solemn rest, a holy convocation. You shall do no work on it; it is the Sabbath of the LORD in all your dwellings.

   Exodus 20:8, 10 Remember the Sabbath day, to keep it holy. [10]But the seventh day is the Sabbath of the LORD your God. In it you shall do no work: you, nor your son, nor your daughter, nor your manservant, nor your maidservant, nor your cattle, nor your stranger who is within your gates.

   Exodus 16:25-28 Then Moses said, Eat that today, for today is a Sabbath to the LORD; today you will not find it in the field. [26]Six days you shall gather it, but on the seventh day, which is the Sabbath, there will be none. [27]Now it happened that some of the people went out on the seventh day to gather, but they found none. [28]And the LORD said to Moses, How long do you refuse to keep My commandments and My laws?

2. *Nehemiah 13:15-22* In those days I saw in Judah some people treading wine presses on the Sabbath, and bringing in sheaves, and loading donkeys with wine, grapes, figs, and all kinds of burdens, which they brought into Jerusalem on the Sabbath day. And I warned them about the day on which they were selling provisions. [16]Men of Tyre dwelt there also, who brought in fish and all kinds of goods, and sold them on the Sabbath to the children of Judah, and in Jerusalem. [17]Then I contended with the nobles of Judah, and said to them, What evil thing is this that you do, by which you profane the Sabbath day? [18]Did not your fathers do thus, and did not our God bring all this disaster on us and on this city? Yet you bring added wrath on Israel by profaning the Sabbath. [19]So it was, at the gates of Jerusalem, as it began to be dark before the Sabbath, that I commanded the gates to be shut, and charged that they must not be opened till after the Sabbath. Then I posted some of my servants at the gates, so that no burdens would be brought in on the Sabbath day. [20]Now the merchants and sellers of all kinds of wares lodged outside Jerusalem once or twice. [21]So I warned them, and said to them, Why do you spend the night around the wall? If you do so again, I will lay hands on you! From that time on they came no more on the Sabbath. [22]And I commanded the Levites that they should cleanse themselves, and that they should go and guard the gates, to sanctify the Sabbath day. Remember me, O my God, concerning this also, and spare me according to the greatness of Your mercy!

3. *Luke 4:16* So He came to Nazareth, where He had been brought up. And as His custom was, He went into the synagogue on the Sabbath day, and stood up to read.

   Acts 20:7 Now on the first day of the week, when the disciples came together to break bread, Paul, ready to depart the next day, spoke to them and continued his message until midnight.

Psalm 92:1-2 (A Psalm, a Song for the Sabbath day.) It is good to give thanks to the LORD, and to sing praises to Your name, O Most High; ²to declare Your lovingkindness in the morning, and Your faithfulness every night.

Isaiah 66:23 And it shall come to pass that from one New Moon to another, and from one Sabbath to another, all flesh shall come to worship before Me, says the LORD.

4. *Matthew 12:11-12* Then He said to them, What man is there among you who has one sheep, and if it falls into a pit on the Sabbath, will not lay hold of it and lift it out? ¹²Of how much more value then is a man than a sheep? Therefore it is lawful to do good on the Sabbath.

64. What is forbidden in the fourth commandment?

The fourth commandment forbids the omission or careless performance of the duties required,¹ and the profaning the day by idleness, or doing that which is in itself sinful,² or by unnecessary thoughts, words, or works, about our worldly employments or recreations.³

1. *Ezekiel 22:26* Her priests have violated My law and profaned My holy things; they have not distinguished between the holy and unholy, nor have they made known the difference between the unclean and the clean; and they have hidden their eyes from My Sabbaths, so that I am profaned among them.

   Amos 8:5 Saying: When will the New Moon be past, that we may sell grain? And the Sabbath, that we may trade our wheat? Making the ephah small and the shekel large, falsifying the balances by deceit.

   Malachi 1:13 You also say, Oh, what a weariness! and you sneer at it, says the LORD of hosts. And you bring the stolen, the lame, and the sick; thus you bring an offering! Should I accept this from your hand? says the LORD.

2. *Ezekiel 23:38* Moreover they have done this to Me: They have defiled My sanctuary on the same day and profaned My Sabbaths.

3. *Jeremiah 17:24-26* And it shall be, if you diligently heed Me, says the LORD, to bring no burden through the gates of this city on the Sabbath day, but hallow the Sabbath day, to do no work in it, ²⁵then shall enter the gates of this city kings and princes sitting on the throne of David, riding in chariots and on horses, they and their princes, accompanied by the men of Judah and the inhabitants of Jerusalem; and this city shall remain forever. ²⁶And they shall come from the cities of Judah and from the places around Jerusalem, from the land of Benjamin and from the lowland, from the mountains and from the South, bringing burnt offerings and sacrifices, grain offerings and incense, bringing sacrifices of praise to the house of the LORD.

   Isaiah 58:13 If you turn away your foot from the Sabbath, from doing your pleasure on My holy day, and call the Sabbath a delight, the holy day of the LORD honorable, and shall honor Him, not doing your own ways, nor finding your own pleasure, nor speaking your own words.

65. What are the reasons annexed to the fourth commandment?

The reasons annexed to the fourth commandment are God's allowing us six days of the week for our own employments,¹ His claiming a special right to the seventh,² His own example,³ and His blessing the Sabbath day.⁴

1. *Exodus 20:9* Six days you shall labor and do all your work.

29

Exodus 31:15-16 Work shall be done for six days, but the seventh is the Sabbath of rest, holy to the LORD. Whoever does any work on the Sabbath day, he shall surely be put to death. ¹⁶Therefore the children of Israel shall keep the Sabbath, to observe the Sabbath throughout their generations as a perpetual covenant.

2. *Exodus 20:10a* But the seventh day is the Sabbath of the LORD your God.

Leviticus 23:3 Six days shall work be done, but the seventh day is a Sabbath of solemn rest, a holy convocation. You shall do no work on it; it is the Sabbath of the LORD in all your dwellings.

3. *Exodus 31:17* It is a sign between Me and the children of Israel forever; for in six days the LORD made the heavens and the earth, and on the seventh day He rested and was refreshed.

4. *Genesis 2:3* Then God blessed the seventh day and sanctified it, because in it He rested from all His work which God had created and made.

Exodus 20:12 For in six days the LORD made the heavens and the earth, the sea, and all that is in them, and rested the seventh day. Therefore the LORD blessed the Sabbath day and hallowed it.

66. What is the fifth commandment?

The fifth commandment is, Honor your father and your mother, that your days may be long upon the land which the LORD your God is giving you.[1]

1. *Exodus 20:12*

67. What is required in the fifth commandment?

The fifth commandment requires the preserving the honor of, and performing the duties belonging to, every one in their several places and relations, as superiors, inferiors, or equals.[1]

1. *Romans 12:10* Be kindly affectionate to one another with brotherly love, in honor giving preference to one another.

Romans 13:1 Let every soul be subject to the governing authorities. For there is no authority except from God, and the authorities that exist are appointed by God.

Ephesians 5:21-23 Submitting to one another in the fear of God. ²²Wives, submit to your own husbands, as to the Lord. ²³For the husband is head of the wife, as also Christ is head of the church; and He is the Savior of the body.

Ephesians 6:1-2, 5 Children, obey your parents in the Lord, for this is right. ²Honor your father and mother, which is the first commandment with promise. ⁵Servants, be obedient to those who are your masters according to the flesh, with fear and trembling, in sincerity of heart, as to Christ.

Ephesians 6:9 And you, masters, do the same things to them, giving up threatening, knowing that your own Master also is in heaven, and there is no partiality with Him.

1 Peter 2:13-14, 17 Therefore submit yourselves to every ordinance of man for the Lord's sake, whether to the king as supreme, ¹⁴or to governors, as to those who are sent by him for the punishment of evildoers and for the praise of those who do good. ¹⁷Honor all people. Love the brotherhood. Fear God. Honor the king.

68. What is forbidden in the fifth commandment?

The fifth commandment forbids the neglecting of, or doing anything against, the honor and duty which belongs to every one in their several places and relations.[1]

1. *Romans 13:7-8* Render therefore to all their due: taxes to whom taxes are due, customs to whom customs, fear to whom fear, honor to whom honor. [8]Owe no one anything except to love one another, for he who loves another has fulfilled the law.

   Matthew 15:4-6 For God commanded, saying, Honor your father and your mother; and, He who curses father or mother, let him be put to death. [5]But you say, Whoever says to his father or mother, Whatever profit you might have received from me has been dedicated to the temple—[6]is released from honoring his father or mother. Thus you have made the commandment of God of no effect by your tradition.

   Ezekiel 34:2 Son of man, prophesy against the shepherds of Israel, prophesy and say to them, Thus says the Lord God to the shepherds: Woe to the shepherds of Israel who feed themselves! Should not the shepherds feed the flocks? [3]You eat the fat and clothe yourselves with the wool; you slaughter the fatlings, but you do not feed the flock. [4]The weak you have not strengthened, nor have you healed those who were sick, nor bound up the broken, nor brought back what was driven away, nor sought what was lost; but with force and cruelty you have ruled them.

69. What is the reason annexed to the fifth commandment?

The reason annexed to the fifth commandment is a promise of long life and prosperity (as far as it shall serve for God's glory and their own good) to all such as keep this commandment.[1]

1. *Deuteronomy 5:16* Honor your father and your mother, as the LORD your God has commanded you, that your days may be long, and that it may be well with you in the land which the LORD your God is giving you.

   Ephesians 6:2-3 Honor your father and mother, which is the first commandment with promise: [3]that it may be well with you and you may live long on the earth.

70. What is the sixth commandment?

The sixth commandment is, You shall not murder.[1]

1. *Exodus 20:13*

71. What is required in the sixth commandment?

The sixth commandment requires all lawful endeavors to preserve our own life,[1] and the life of others.[2]

1. *Ephesians 5:28-29* So husbands ought to love their own wives as their own bodies; he who loves his wife loves himself. [29]For no one ever hated his own flesh, but nourishes and cherishes it, just as the Lord does the church.
2. *Psalm 82:3-4* Defend the poor and fatherless; do justice to the afflicted and needy. [4]Deliver the poor and needy; free them from the hand of the wicked.

   Job 29:13 The blessing of a perishing man came upon me, and I caused the widow's heart to sing for joy.

1 Kings 18:4 For so it was, while Jezebel massacred the prophets of the LORD, that Obadiah had taken one hundred prophets and hidden them, fifty to a cave, and had fed them with bread and water.

72. What is forbidden in the sixth commandment?

The sixth commandment forbids the taking away of our own life,[1] or the life of our neighbor unjustly,[2] or whatsoever tends thereunto.[3]

1. *Acts 16:28* But Paul called with a loud voice, saying, Do yourself no harm, for we are all here.
2. *Genesis 9:6* Whoever sheds man's blood, by man his blood shall be shed; for in the image of God He made man.
3. *Leviticus 19:17* You shall not hate your brother in your heart. You shall surely rebuke your neighbor, and not bear sin because of him.
   Proverbs 24:11-12 Deliver those who are drawn toward death, and hold back those stumbling to the slaughter. [12]If you say, Surely we did not know this, does not He who weighs the hearts consider it? He who keeps your soul, does He not know it? and will He not render to each man according to his deeds?

73. What is the seventh commandment?

The seventh commandment is, You shall not commit adultery.[1]

1. *Exodus 20:14*

74. What is required in the seventh commandment?

The seventh commandment requires the preservation of our own and our neighbor's chastity,[1] in heart,[2] speech,[3] and behavior.[4]

1. *1 Thessalonians 4:3-5* For this is the will of God, your sanctification: that you should abstain from sexual immorality; [4]that each of you should know how to possess his own vessel in sanctification and honor, [5]not in passion of lust, like the Gentiles who do not know God.
   1 Corinthians 7:2 Nevertheless, because of sexual immorality, let each man have his own wife, and let each woman have her own husband. [3]Let the husband render to his wife the affection due her, and likewise also the wife to her husband. [4]The wife does not have authority over her own body, but the husband does. And likewise the husband does not have authority over his own body, but the wife does. [5]Do not deprive one another except with consent for a time, that you may give yourselves to fasting and prayer; and come together again so that Satan does not tempt you because of your lack of self-control.
   Ephesians 5:11-12 And have no fellowship with the unfruitful works of darkness, but rather expose them. [12]For it is shameful even to speak of those things which are done by them in secret.
2. *2 Timothy 2:22* Flee also youthful lusts; but pursue righteousness, faith, love, peace with those who call on the Lord out of a pure heart.
3. *Ephesians 5:4* But fornication and all uncleanness or covetousness, let it not even be named among you, as is fitting for saints; [4]Neither filthiness, nor foolish talking, nor coarse jesting, which are not fitting, but rather giving of thanks.
4. *1 Peter 3:2* When they observe your chaste conduct accompanied by fear.

75. What is forbidden in the seventh commandment?

The seventh commandment forbids all unchaste thoughts,[1] words, and actions.[2]

1. *Matthew 15:19* For out of the heart proceed evil thoughts, murders, adulteries, fornications, thefts, false witness, blasphemies.

   Matthew 5:28 But I say to you that whoever looks at a woman to lust for her has already committed adultery with her in his heart.

2. *Ephesians 5:3-4* But fornication and all uncleanness or covetousness, let it not even be named among you, as is fitting for saints; ⁴neither filthiness, nor foolish talking, nor coarse jesting, which are not fitting, but rather giving of thanks.

76. What is the eighth commandment?

The eighth commandment is, You shall not steal.[1]

1. *Exodus 20:15*

77. What is required in the eighth commandment?

The eighth commandment requires the lawful procuring and furthering the wealth and outward estate of ourselves and others.[1]

1. *1 Timothy 5:8* But if anyone does not provide for his own, and especially for those of his household, he has denied the faith and is worse than an unbeliever.

   Proverbs 27:23 Be diligent to know the state of your flocks, and attend to your herds.

   Acts 20:33-35 I have coveted no one's silver or gold or apparel. ³⁴Yes, you yourselves know that these hands have provided for my necessities, and for those who were with me. ³⁵I have shown you in every way, by laboring like this, that you must support the weak. And remember the words of the Lord Jesus, that He said, It is more blessed to give than to receive.

   Philippians 2:4 Let each of you look out not only for his own interests, but also for the interests of others.

   Leviticus 25:35 And if one of your brethren becomes poor, and falls into poverty among you, then you shall help him, like a stranger or a sojourner, that he may live with you.

   Deuteronomy 22:1-4 You shall not see your brother's ox or his sheep going astray, and hide yourself from them; you shall certainly bring them back to your brother. ²And if your brother is not near you, or if you do not know him, then you shall bring it to your own house, and it shall remain with you until your brother seeks it; then you shall restore it to him. ³You shall do the same with his donkey, and so shall you do with his garment; with any lost thing of your brother's, which he has lost and you have found, you shall do likewise; you must not hide yourself. ⁴You shall not see your brother's donkey or his ox fall down along the road, and hide yourself from them; you shall surely help him lift them up again.

   Exodus 23:4-5 If you meet your enemy's ox or his donkey going astray, you shall surely bring it back to him again. ⁵If you see the donkey of one who hates you lying under its burden, and you would refrain from helping it, you shall surely help him with it.

   Job 29:11-17 When the ear heard, then it blessed me, and when the eye saw, then it approved me; ¹²because I delivered the poor who cried out, and the fatherless and he who had no helper. ¹³The blessing of a perishing man came upon me, and I caused the widow's heart to sing for joy. ¹⁴I put on righteousness, and it clothed me; my justice was like a robe and a turban. ¹⁵I was eyes to the blind, and I was feet to the lame. ¹⁶I was a father to the poor, and I searched out the case that I did not know. [17]I broke the fangs of the wicked, and plucked the victim from his teeth.

78. What is forbidden in the eighth commandment?

The eighth commandment forbids whatsoever does, or may, unjustly hinder our own, or our neighbor's, wealth or outward estate.[1]

1. *Proverbs 21:17* He who loves pleasure will be a poor man; he who loves wine and oil will not be rich.

   Proverbs 23:20-21 Do not mix with winebibbers, or with gluttonous eaters of meat; [21]for the drunkard and the glutton will come to poverty, and drowsiness will clothe a man with rags.

   Proverbs 28:19 He who tills his land will have plenty of bread, but he who follows frivolity will have poverty enough!

   Ephesians 4:28 Let him who stole steal no longer, but rather let him labor, working with his hands what is good, that he may have something to give him who has need.

79. What is the ninth commandment?

The ninth commandment is, You shall not bear false witness against your neighbor.[1]

1. *Exodus 20:16*

80. What is required in the ninth commandment?

The ninth commandment requires the maintaining and promoting of truth between man and man,[1] and of our own[2] and our neighbor's good name,[3] especially in witness-bearing.[4]

1. *Zechariah 8:16* These are the things you shall do: speak each man the truth to his neighbor; give judgment in your gates for truth, justice, and peace.
2. *1 Peter 3:16* Having a good conscience, that when they defame you as evildoers, those who revile your good conduct in Christ may be ashamed.

   Acts 25:10 Then Paul said, I stand at Caesar's judgment seat, where I ought to be judged. To the Jews I have done no wrong, as you very well know.
3. *3 John 12* Demetrius has a good testimony from all, and from the truth itself. And we also bear witness, and you know that our testimony is true.
4. *Proverbs 14:5, 25* A faithful witness does not lie, but a false witness will utter lies. [25]A true witness delivers souls, but a deceitful witness speaks lies.

81. What is forbidden in the ninth commandment?

The ninth commandment forbids whatsoever is prejudicial to truth,[1] or injurious to our own[2] or our neighbor's good name.[3]

1. *Romans 3:13* Their throat is an open tomb; with their tongues they have practiced deceit; The poison of asps is under their lips.
2. *Job 27:5* Far be it from me that I should say you are right; till I die I will not put away my integrity from me.
3. *Leviticus 19:16* You shall not go about as a talebearer among your people; nor shall you take a stand against the life of your neighbor: I am the LORD.

Psalm 15:3 He who does not backbite with his tongue, nor does evil to his neighbor, nor does he take up a reproach against his friend.

82. What is the tenth commandment?

You shall not covet your neighbor's house; you shall not covet your neighbor's wife, nor his manservant, nor his maidservant, nor his ox, nor his donkey, nor anything that is your neighbor's.[1]

1. *Exodus 20:17*

83. What is required in the tenth commandment?

The tenth commandment requires full contentment with our own condition,[1] with a right and charitable frame of spirit toward our neighbor, and all that is his.[2]

1. *Hebrews 13:5* Let your conduct be without covetousness, and be content with such things as you have. For He Himself has said, I will never leave you nor forsake you.

   1 Timothy 6:6 But godliness with contentment is great gain.

2. *Job 31:29-30* If I have rejoiced at the destruction of him who hated me, or lifted myself up when evil found him [30](Indeed I have not allowed my mouth to sin by asking for a curse on his soul).

   Romans 12:15 Rejoice with those who rejoice, and weep with those who weep.

   1 Timothy 1:5 Now the purpose of the commandment is love from a pure heart, from a good conscience, and from sincere faith.

   1 Corinthians 13:4-7 Love suffers long and is kind; love does not envy; love does not parade itself, is not puffed up; [5]does not behave rudely, does not seek its own, is not provoked, thinks no evil; [6]does not rejoice in iniquity, but rejoices in the truth; [7]bears all things, believes all things, hopes all things, endures all things.

84. What is forbidden in the tenth commandment?

The tenth commandment forbids all discontentment with our own estate,[1] envying or grieving at the good of our neighbor,[2] and all inordinate motions and affections to any thing that is his.[3]

1. *1 Kings 21:4* So Ahab went into his house sullen and displeased because of the word which Naboth the Jezreelite had spoken to him; for he had said, I will not give you the inheritance of my fathers. And he lay down on his bed, and turned away his face, and would eat no food.

   Esther 5:13 Yet all this avails me nothing, so long as I see Mordecai the Jew sitting at the king's gate.

   1 Corinthians 10:10 Nor murmur, as some of them also murmured, and were destroyed by the destroyer.

2. *Galatians 5:26* Let us not become conceited, provoking one another, envying one another.

   James 3:14, 16 But if you have bitter envy and self-seeking in your hearts, do not boast and lie against the truth. [16]For where envy and self-seeking exist, confusion and every evil thing will be there.

3. *Colossians 3:5* Therefore put to death your members which are on the earth: fornication, uncleanness, passion, evil desire, and covetousness, which is idolatry.

85. Is any man able perfectly to keep the commandments of God?

No mere man since the fall is able, in this life, perfectly to keep the commandments of God;[1] but daily breaks them in thought, word, and deed.[2]

1. *Ecclesiastes 7:20* For there is not a just man on earth who does good and does not sin.

   1 John 1:8, 10 If we say that we have no sin, we deceive ourselves, and the truth is not in us. [10]If we say that we have not sinned, we make Him a liar, and His word is not in us.

   Galatians 5:17 For the flesh lusts against the Spirit, and the Spirit against the flesh; and these are contrary to one another, so that you do not do the things that you wish.

2. *Genesis 6:5* Then the LORD saw that the wickedness of man was great in the earth, and that every intent of the thoughts of his heart was only evil continually.

   Genesis 8:21 And the LORD smelled a soothing aroma. Then the LORD said in His heart, I will never again curse the ground for man's sake, although the imagination of man's heart is evil from his youth; nor will I again destroy every living thing as I have done.

   Romans 3:9-20 What then? Are we better than they? Not at all. For we have previously charged both Jews and Greeks that they are all under sin. . . .

   James 3:2-12 For we all stumble in many things. If anyone does not stumble in word, he is a perfect man, able also to bridle the whole body. . . . [8]But no man can tame the tongue. It is an unruly evil, full of deadly poison. . . .

86. Are all transgressions of the law equally heinous?

Some sins in themselves, and by reason of several aggravations, are more heinous in the sight of God than others.[1]

1. *Ezekiel 8:6, 13, 15* Furthermore He said to me, Son of man, do you see what they are doing, the great abominations that the house of Israel commits here, to make Me go far away from My sanctuary? Now turn again, you will see greater abominations. [13]And He said to me, Turn again, and you will see greater abominations that they are doing. [15]Then He said to me, Have you seen this, O son of man? Turn again, you will see greater abominations than these.

   John 19:11 Jesus answered, You could have no power at all against Me unless it had been given you from above. Therefore the one who delivered Me to you has the greater sin.

87. What does every sin deserve?

Every sin deserves God's wrath and curse, both in this life and that which is to come.[1]

1. *Ephesians 5:6* Let no one deceive you with empty words, for because of these things the wrath of God comes upon the sons of disobedience.

   Galatians 3:10 For as many as are of the works of the law are under the curse; for it is written, Cursed is everyone who does not continue in all things which are written in the book of the law, to do them.

   Lamentations 3:39 Why should a living man complain, a man for the punishment of his sins?

   Matthew 25:41 Then He will also say to those on the left hand, Depart from Me, you cursed, into the everlasting fire prepared for the devil and his angels.

88. What way of escape has God revealed to sinners that they may be saved from His wrath and curse due to them for their sin?

God has revealed to sinners the gospel of His Son, Jesus Christ, as the only way of salvation from their sins.

1. *Romans 1:16* For I am not ashamed of the gospel of Christ, for it is the power of God to salvation for everyone who believes, for the Jew first and also for the Greek.

   Acts 4:12 Nor is there salvation in any other, for there is no other name under heaven given among men by which we must be saved.

89. What does God, in His gospel, require of sinners that they may be saved?

God, in His gospel, requires of sinners faith in Jesus Christ and repentance unto life that they may escape His wrath due for their sin, and be saved.[1]

1. *Acts 20:21* Testifying to Jews, and also to Greeks, repentance toward God and faith toward our Lord Jesus Christ.

90. What is faith in Jesus Christ?

Faith in Jesus Christ is a saving grace,[1] whereby sinners receive[2] and rest upon Him alone for salvation,[3] as He is offered to them in the gospel.[4]

1. *Ephesians 2:8-9* For by grace you have been saved through faith, and that not of yourselves; it is the gift of God, 9not of works, lest anyone should boast.
2. *John 1:12* But as many as received Him, to them He gave the right to become children of God, even to those who believe in His name.
3. *Philippians 3:9* And be found in Him, not having my own righteousness, which is from the law, but that which is through faith in Christ, the righteousness which is from God by faith.

   Galatians 2:16 Knowing that a man is not justified by the works of the law but by faith in Jesus Christ, even we have believed in Christ Jesus, that we might be justified by faith in Christ and not by the works of the law; for by the works of the law no flesh shall be justified.
4. *Romans 10:14, 17* How then shall they call on Him in whom they have not believed? And how shall they believe in Him of whom they have not heard? And how shall they hear without a preacher? 17So then faith comes by hearing, and hearing by the word of God.

91. What is repentance unto life?

Repentance unto life is a saving grace,[1] whereby a sinner, out of a true sense of his sin,[2] and apprehension of the mercy of God in Christ,[3] does, with grief and hatred of his sin, turn from it unto God,[4] with full purpose of, and endeavor after, new obedience.[5]

1. *Acts 11:18* When they heard these things they became silent; and they glorified God, saying, Then God has also granted to the Gentiles repentance to life.

2. *Acts 2:37-38* Now when they heard this, they were cut to the heart, and said to Peter and the rest of the apostles, Men and brethren, what shall we do? [38]Then Peter said to them, Repent, and let every one of you be baptized in the name of Jesus Christ for the remission of sins; and you shall receive the gift of the Holy Spirit.

3. *Joel 2:12-13* Now, therefore, says the LORD, Turn to me with all your heart, with fasting, with weeping, and with mourning. [13]So rend your heart, and not your garments; return to the LORD your God, for He is gracious and merciful, slow to anger, and of great kindness; and He relents from doing harm.

4. *Jeremiah 31:18-19* I have surely heard Ephraim bemoaning himself: You have chastised me, and I was chastised, like an untrained bull; restore me, and I will return, for You are the LORD my God. [19]Surely, after my turning, I repented; and after I was instructed, I struck myself on the thigh; I was ashamed, yes, even humiliated, because I bore the reproach of my youth.

   Ezekiel 36:31 Then you will remember your evil ways and your deeds that were not good; and you will loathe yourselves in your own sight, for your iniquities and your abominations.

5. *Psalm 119:59* I thought about my ways, and turned my feet to Your testimonies.

92. Will all who outwardly profess obedience to the gospel escape the wrath due for their sins?

Not all who outwardly profess obedience to the gospel,[1] but only those who persevere in faith and holiness to the end shall be saved.[2]

1. *Matthew 7:21* Not everyone who says to Me, Lord, Lord, shall enter the kingdom of heaven, but he who does the will of My Father in heaven.

2. *1 Peter 1:5* Who are kept by the power of God through faith for salvation ready to be revealed in the last time.

   Hebrews 12:14 Pursue peace with all men, and holiness, without which no one will see the Lord.

93. Who then will persevere in faith and holiness unto the end and be saved?

All true believers, by reason of God's eternal decree and unchangeable love,[1] Christ's intercession,[2] and the Spirit and word of God abiding in them,[3] are preserved by the power of God[4] and supplied with every spiritual blessing in Christ,[5] and therefore will most certainly persevere in faith and holiness unto the end and be saved.[6]

1. *Romans 8:28-30* And we know that all things work together for good to those who love God, to those who are the called according to His purpose. [29]For whom He foreknew, He also predestined to be conformed to the image of His Son, that He might be the firstborn among many brethren. [30]Moreover whom He predestined, these He also called; whom He called, these He also justified; and whom He justified, these He also glorified.

   Jeremiah 31:3 The LORD has appeared of old to me, saying: Yes, I have loved you with an everlasting love; therefore with lovingkindness I have drawn you.

2. *Hebrews 7:25* Therefore He is also able to save to the uttermost those who come to God through Him, since He ever lives to make intercession for them.

3. *John 14:16* And I will pray the Father, and He will give you another Helper, that He may abide with you forever.

4. *John 10:28-29* And I give them eternal life, and they shall never perish; neither shall anyone snatch them out of My hand. ²⁹My Father, who has given them to Me, is greater than all; and no one is able to snatch them out of My Father's hand.

   1 Peter 1:5 Who are kept by the power of God through faith for salvation ready to be revealed in the last time.

5. *Ephesians 1:3* Blessed be the God and Father of our Lord Jesus Christ, who has blessed us with every spiritual blessing in the heavenly places in Christ.

6. *1 Corinthians 1:8-9* Who will also confirm you to the end, that you may be blameless in the day of our Lord Jesus Christ. ⁹God is faithful, by whom you were called into the fellowship of His Son, Jesus Christ our Lord.

   Philippians 1:6 Being confident of this very thing, that He who has begun a good work in you will complete it until the day of Jesus Christ.

94. What are the outward and ordinary means of grace whereby God preserves his elect and communicates to them the blessings of redemption in Christ?

The outward and ordinary means of grace whereby God preserves his elect and communicates to them the blessings of redemption in Christ are his ordinances, especially the word, the sacraments, and prayer;[1] all which are made effectual to the elect for salvation.

1. *Matthew 28:19-20* Go therefore and make disciples of all the nations, baptizing them in the name of the Father and of the Son and of the Holy Spirit, ²⁰teaching them to observe all things that I have commanded you; and lo, I am with you always, even to the end of the age. Amen.

   Acts 2:41-42, 46-47 Then those who gladly received his word were baptized; and that day about three thousand souls were added to them. ⁴²And they continued steadfastly in the apostles' doctrine and fellowship, in the breaking of bread, and in prayers. ⁴⁶So continuing daily with one accord in the temple, and breaking bread from house to house, they ate their food with gladness and simplicity of heart, ⁴⁷praising God and having favor with all the people. And the Lord added to the church daily those who were being saved.

95. How is the word made effectual to salvation?

The Spirit of God makes the reading,[1] but especially the preaching of the word,[2] an effectual means of convincing and converting sinners[3] and of building up believers in holiness and comfort[4] through faith unto salvation.[5]

1. *Nehemiah 8:8* So they read distinctly from the book, in the Law of God; and they gave the sense, and helped them to understand the reading.

   1 Timothy 4:13, 16 Till I come, give attention to reading, to exhortation, to doctrine. ¹⁶Take heed to yourself and to the doctrine. Continue in them, for in doing this you will save both yourself and those who hear you.

2. *1 Corinthians 1:21* For since, in the wisdom of God, the world through wisdom did not know God, it pleased God through the foolishness of the message preached to save those who believe.

Romans 10:13-17 For Whoever calls upon the name of the LORD shall be saved. [14]How then shall they call on Him in whom they have not believed? And how shall they believe in Him of whom they have not heard? And how shall they hear without a preacher? [15]And how shall they preach unless they are sent? As it is written: How beautiful are the feet of those who preach the gospel of peace, who bring glad tidings of good things! [16]But they have not all obeyed the gospel. For Isaiah says, Lord, who has believed our report? [17]So then faith comes by hearing, and hearing by the word of God.

3. *Psalm 19:7-8* The law of the LORD is perfect, converting the soul; the testimony of the LORD is sure, making wise the simple. [8]The statutes of the LORD are right, rejoicing the heart; the commandment of the LORD is pure, enlightening the eyes.

1 Corinthians 14:24-25 But if all prophesy, and an unbeliever or an uninformed person comes in, he is convinced by all, he is judged by all. [25]And thus the secrets of his heart are revealed; and so, falling down on his face, he will worship God and report that God is truly among you.

4. *Acts 20:32* And now, brethren, I commend you to God and to the word of His grace, which is able to build you up and give you an inheritance among all those who are sanctified.

Romans 15:4 For whatever things were written before were written for our learning, that we through the patience and comfort of the Scriptures might have hope.

1 Thessalonians 1:6 And you became followers of us and of the Lord, having received the word in much affliction, with joy of the Holy Spirit.

5. *Romans 1:16* For I am not ashamed of the gospel of Christ, for it is the power of God to salvation for everyone who believes, for the Jew first and also for the Greek.

2 Timothy 3:15-17 And that from childhood you have known the Holy Scriptures, which are able to make you wise for salvation through faith which is in Christ Jesus. [16]All Scripture is given by inspiration of God, and is profitable for doctrine, for reproof, for correction, for instruction in righteousness, [17]that the man of God may be complete, thoroughly equipped for every good work.

96. How is the word to be read and heard, that it may become effectual to salvation?

That the word may become effectual to salvation, the hearers of the word must attend thereunto with diligence,[1] preparation,[2] and prayer;[3] receive it with faith[4] and love,[5] lay it up in their hearts,[6] and practice it in their lives.[7]

1. *Proverbs 8:34* Blessed is the man who listens to me, watching daily at my gates, waiting at the posts of my doors.
2. *1 Peter 2:1-2* Therefore, laying aside all malice, all guile, hypocrisy, envy, and all evil speaking, [2]as newborn babes, desire the pure milk of the word, that you may grow thereby.
3. *Psalm 119:18* Open my eyes, that I may see wondrous things from Your law.
4. *Hebrews 4:2* For indeed the gospel was preached to us as well as to them; but the word which they heard did not profit them, not being mixed with faith in those who heard it.
5. *2 Thessalonians 2:10* And with all unrighteous deception among those who perish, because they did not receive the love of the truth, that they might be saved.
6. *Psalm 119:11* Your word I have hidden in my heart, That I might not sin against You.
7. *Luke 8:15* But the ones that fell on the good ground are those who, having heard the word with a noble and good heart, keep it and bear fruit with patience.

James 1:25 But he who looks into the perfect law of liberty and continues in it, and is not a forgetful hearer but a doer of the work, this one will be blessed in what he does.

97. What is a sacrament of the new covenant?

A sacrament of the new covenant is a holy ritual instituted by Jesus Christ; wherein, by sensible signs, Christ and the benefits of the new covenant are represented, sealed, and applied to believers.[1]

1. *1 Corinthians 11:23-26* For I received from the Lord that which I also delivered to you: that the Lord Jesus on the same night in which He was betrayed took bread; [24]and when He had given thanks, He broke it and said, Take, eat; this is My body which is broken for you; do this in remembrance of Me. [25]In the same manner He also took the cup after supper, saying, This cup is the new covenant in My blood. This do, as often as you drink it, in remembrance of Me. [26]For as often as you eat this bread and drink this cup, you proclaim the Lord's death till He comes.

98. What are the sacraments of the new covenant?

The sacraments of the new covenant are baptism[1] and the Lord's supper.[2]

1. *Matthew 28:19* Go therefore and make disciples of all the nations, baptizing them in the name of the Father and of the Son and of the Holy Spirit.
2. *1 Corinthians 11:23-26* For I received from the Lord that which I also delivered to you: that the Lord Jesus on the same night in which He was betrayed took bread; [24]and when He had given thanks, He broke it and said, Take, eat; this is My body which is broken for you; do this in remembrance of Me. [25]In the same manner He also took the cup after supper, saying, This cup is the new covenant in My blood. This do, as often as you drink it, in remembrance of Me. [26]For as often as you eat this bread and drink this cup, you proclaim the Lord's death till He comes.

99. How do baptism and the Lord's supper become effectual means of salvation?

Baptism and the Lord's supper become effectual means of salvation, not from any virtue in them, or in him that administers them;[1] but only by the blessing of Christ, and the working of His Spirit in those who by faith receive them.[2]

1. *1 Corinthians 3:6-7* I planted, Apollos watered, but God gave the increase. [7]So then neither he who plants is anything, nor he who waters, but God who gives the increase.
2. *1 Peter 3:21* There is also an antitype which now saves us, namely baptism (not the removal of the filth of the flesh, but the answer of a good conscience toward God), through the resurrection of Jesus Christ.

100. What is baptism?

Baptism is a sacrament of the new covenant instituted by Jesus Christ,[1] to be unto the person baptized a sign of his fellowship with Him, in His death, burial, and resurrection; of his being ingrafted into Him; of remission of sins; and of his giving up himself unto God through Jesus Christ, to live and walk in newness of life.[2]

1. *Matthew 28:19* Go therefore and make disciples of all the nations, baptizing them in the name of the Father and of the Son and of the Holy Spirit.

2. *Romans 6:3-4* Or do you not know that as many of us as were baptized into Christ Jesus were baptized into His death? ⁴Therefore we were buried with Him through baptism into death, that just as Christ was raised from the dead by the glory of the Father, even so we also should walk in newness of life.

   Colossians 2:12 Buried with Him in baptism, in which you also were raised with Him through faith in the working of God, who raised Him from the dead.

   Galatians 3:26-27 For you are all sons of God through faith in Christ Jesus. ²⁷For as many of you as were baptized into Christ have put on Christ.

101. To whom is baptism to be administered?

Baptism is to be administered to all those who credibly profess repentance towards God,[1] faith in and obedience to our Lord Jesus Christ,[2] and to none other.

1. *Acts 2:38* Then Peter said to them, Repent, and let every one of you be baptized in the name of Jesus Christ for the remission of sins; and you shall receive the gift of the Holy Spirit.

   Acts 2:41 Then those who gladly received his word were baptized; and that day about three thousand souls were added to them.

2. *Mark 16:16* He who believes and is baptized will be saved; but he who does not believe will be condemned.

   Acts 8:12 But when they believed Philip as he preached the things concerning the kingdom of God and the name of Jesus Christ, both men and women were baptized.

102. Are the infants of professing believers to be baptized?

The infants of professing believers are not to be baptized, because there is neither command nor example in the Holy Scriptures, nor certain inference from them, to baptize such.[1]

1. *Deuteronomy 12:32* Whatever I command you, be careful to observe it; you shall not add to it nor take away from it.

   Proverbs 30:6 Do not add to His words, lest He reprove you, and you be found a liar.

   Acts 8:12 But when they believed Philip as he preached the things concerning the kingdom of God and the name of Jesus Christ, both men and women were baptized.

   Acts 10:47-48 Can anyone forbid water, that these should not be baptized who have received the Holy Spirit just as we have? ⁴⁸And he commanded them to be baptized in the name of the Lord. Then they asked him to stay a few days.

103. How is baptism rightly administered?

Baptism is rightly administered by immersion, or dipping the whole body of the believer in water, in the name of the Father, and of the Son, and of the Holy Spirit, according to Christ's institution,[1] and the practice of the apostles,[2] and not by sprinkling or pouring of water, or dipping some part of the body, after the tradition of men.

1. *Matthew 3:16* Then Jesus, when He had been baptized, came up immediately from the water; and behold, the heavens were opened to Him, and He saw the Spirit of God descending like a dove and alighting upon Him.

   John 3:23 Now John also was baptizing in Aenon near Salim, because there was much water there. And they came and were baptized.

2. *Acts 8:38-39* So he commanded the chariot to stand still. And both Philip and the eunuch went down into the water, and he baptized him. [39]Now when they came up out of the water, the Spirit of the Lord caught Philip away, so that the eunuch saw him no more; and he went on his way rejoicing.

104. What is the Lord's supper?

The Lord's supper is a sacrament of the new covenant, wherein, by giving and receiving bread and fruit of the vine, according to Christ's appointment, His death is shown forth;[1] and the worthy receivers are, not after a corporal and carnal manner, but by faith, made partakers of His body and blood, with all His benefits, to their spiritual nourishment and growth in grace.[2]

1. *1 Corinthians 11:23-26* For I received from the Lord that which I also delivered to you: that the Lord Jesus on the same night in which He was betrayed took bread; [24]and when He had given thanks, He broke it and said, Take, eat; this is My body which is broken for you; do this in remembrance of Me. [25]In the same manner He also took the cup after supper, saying, This cup is the new covenant in My blood. This do, as often as you drink it, in remembrance of Me.[26]For as often as you eat this bread and drink this cup, you proclaim the Lord's death till He comes.

2. *1 Corinthians 10:16* The cup of blessing which we bless, is it not the communion of the blood of Christ? The bread which we break, is it not the communion of the body of Christ?

105. What is required for the worthy receiving of the Lord's supper?

It is required of them that would worthily partake of the Lord's supper, that they examine themselves of their knowledge to discern the Lord's body,[1] of their faith to feed upon Him,[2] of their repentance,[3] love,[4] and new obedience;[5] lest coming unworthily, they eat and drink judgment to themselves.[6]

1. *1 Corinthians 11:28-29* But let a man examine himself, and so let him eat of that bread and drink of that cup. [29]For he who eats and drinks in an unworthy manner eats and drinks judgment to himself, not discerning the Lord's body.

2. *2 Corinthians 13:5* Examine yourselves as to whether you are in the faith. Prove yourselves. Do you not know yourselves, that Jesus Christ is in you?—unless indeed you are disqualified.
3. *1 Corinthians 11:31* For if we would judge ourselves, we would not be judged.
4. *1 Corinthians 11:16-17* But if anyone seems to be contentious, we have no such custom, nor do the churches of God. ¹⁷Now in giving these instructions I do not praise you, since you come together not for the better but for the worse.
5. *1 Corinthians 5:7-8* Therefore purge out the old leaven, that you may be a new lump, since you truly are unleavened. For indeed Christ, our Passover, was sacrificed for us. ⁸Therefore let us keep the feast, not with old leaven, nor with the leaven of malice and wickedness, but with the unleavened bread of sincerity and truth.
6. *1 Corinthians 11:28-29* [See 1. above.]

106. What is prayer which is acceptable to God?

Acceptable prayer is an offering up of the desires of the righteous[1] unto God,[2] for things agreeable to His will,[3] in the name of Christ,[4] by the help of His Spirit,[5] with confession of sins,[6] and thankful acknowledgement of His mercies.[7]

1. *Proverbs 15:8* The sacrifice of the wicked is an abomination to the LORD, but the prayer of the upright is His delight.
   Proverbs 28:9 One who turns away his ear from hearing the law, even his prayer shall be an abomination.
2. *Psalm 62:8* Trust in Him at all times, you people; pour out your heart before Him; God is a refuge for us. Selah
3. *1 John 5:14* Now this is the confidence that we have in Him, that if we ask anything according to His will, He hears us.
4. *John 16:23* And in that day you will ask Me nothing. Most assuredly, I say to you, whatever you ask the Father in My name He will give you.
5. *Romans 8:26* Likewise the Spirit also helps in our weaknesses. For we do not know what we should pray for as we ought, but the Spirit Himself makes intercession for us with groanings which cannot be uttered.
6. *Psalm 32:5-6* I acknowledged my sin to You, and my iniquity I have not hidden. I said, I will confess my transgressions to the LORD, and You forgave the iniquity of my sin. Selah ⁶For this cause everyone who is godly shall pray to You in a time when You may be found; surely in a flood of great waters They shall not come near him.
   Daniel 9:4 And I prayed to the LORD my God, and made confession, and said, O Lord, great and awesome God, who keeps His covenant and mercy with those who love Him, and with those who keep His commandments.
7. *Philippians 4:6* Be anxious for nothing, but in everything by prayer and supplication, with thanksgiving, let your requests be made known to God.

107. What rule has God given for the direction of His people in prayer?

The whole word of God is of use to direct His people in prayer,[1] but the special rule of direction is that pattern of prayer which Christ taught His disciples, commonly called *The Lord's Prayer.*[2]

1. *1 John 5:14* Now this is the confidence that we have in Him, that if we ask anything according to His will, He hears us.
2. *Matthew 6:9-13* In this manner, therefore, pray: Our Father. . . .
   Luke 11:2-4 So He said to them, When you pray, say: Our Father. . . .

108. What does the preface of the Lord's prayer teach His disciples?

The preface of the Lord's prayer (which is, *Our Father in heaven*[1]) teaches His disciples, commonly called Christians,[2] to draw near to God with all holy reverence and confidence, as children to a father, able and ready to help them;[3] and that they should pray with and for others.[4]

1. *Matthew 6:9b*
2. *Acts 11:26c* And the disciples were first called Christians in Antioch.
3. *Isaiah 64:9* Do not be furious, O LORD, nor remember iniquity forever; indeed, please look—we all are Your people!
   Luke 11:13 If you then, being evil, know how to give good gifts to your children, how much more will your heavenly Father give the Holy Spirit to those who ask Him!
   Romans 8:15 For you did not receive the spirit of bondage again to fear, but you received the Spirit of adoption by whom we cry out, Abba, Father.
4. *1 Timothy 2:1-2* Therefore I exhort first of all that supplications, prayers, intercessions, and giving of thanks be made for all men, [2]for kings and all who are in authority, that we may lead a quiet and peaceable life in all godliness and reverence.
   Ephesians 6:18 Praying always with all prayer and supplication in the Spirit, being watchful to this end with all perseverance and supplication for all the saints.

109. What do Christians pray for in the first petition?

In the first petition (which is, *Hallowed be Your name*[1]) Christians pray that God would enable them and others to glorify Him in all that whereby He makes Himself known,[2] and that He would dispose all things to His own glory.[3]

1. *Matthew 6:9c*
2. *Psalm 67:1-3* God be merciful to us and bless us, and cause His face to shine upon us. Selah [2]That Your way may be known on earth, Your salvation among all nations. [3]Let the peoples praise You, O God; let all the peoples praise You.
3. *Romans 11:36* For of Him and through Him and to Him are all things, to whom be glory forever. Amen.

110. What do Christians pray for in the second petition?

In the second petition (which is, *Your kingdom come*[1]) Christians pray that Satan's kingdom may be destroyed,[2] and that the kingdom of grace may be advanced,[3] sinners brought into it,[4] and believers kept in it,[5] and that the kingdom of glory may be hastened.[6]

1. *Matthew 6:10a*

2. *Psalm 68:1* Let God arise, let His enemies be scattered; let those also who hate Him flee before Him.

3. *Psalm 51:18* Do good in Your good pleasure to Zion; build the walls of Jerusalem.

   Revelation 12:10-11 Then I heard a loud voice saying in heaven, Now salvation, and strength, and the kingdom of our God, and the power of His Christ have come, for the accuser of our brethren, who accused them before our God day and night, has been cast down. [11]And they overcame him by the blood of the Lamb and by the word of their testimony, and they did not love their lives to the death.

4. *2 Thessalonians 3:1* Finally, brethren, pray for us, that the word of the Lord may have free course and be glorified, just as it is with you.

   Romans 10:1 Brethren, my heart's desire and prayer to God for Israel is that they may be saved.

5. *Colossians 1:9-13* For this reason we also, since the day we heard it, do not cease to pray for you, and to ask that you may be filled with the knowledge of His will in all wisdom and spiritual understanding; [10]that you may have a walk worthy of the Lord, fully pleasing Him, being fruitful in every good work and increasing in the knowledge of God; [11]strengthened with all might, according to His glorious power, for all patience and longsuffering with joy; [12]giving thanks to the Father who has qualified us to be partakers of the inheritance of the saints in the light. [13]He has delivered us from the power of darkness and translated us into the kingdom of the Son of His love.

6. *Revelation 22:20* He who testifies to these things says, Surely I am coming quickly. Amen. Even so, come, Lord Jesus!

111. What do Christians pray for in the third petition?

In the third petition (which is, *Your will be done on earth as it is in heaven.*[1]) Christians pray that God by His grace would make them able and willing to know,[2] obey,[3] and submit to His will in all things,[4] as the angels do in heaven.[5]

1. *Matthew 6:10b*

2. *Psalm 119:34* Give me understanding, and I shall keep Your law; indeed, I shall observe it with my whole heart.

3. *Psalm 119:35-36* Make me walk in the path of Your commandments, for I delight in it. [36]Incline my heart to Your testimonies, and not to covetousness.

4. *Job 1:21* And he said: Naked I came from my mother's womb, and naked shall I return there. The LORD gave, and the LORD has taken away; blessed be the name of the LORD.

   Acts 21:14 So when he would not be persuaded, we ceased, saying, The will of the Lord be done.

5. *Psalm 103:20-21* Bless the LORD, you His angels, who excel in strength, who do His word, heeding the voice of His word. [21]Bless the LORD, all you His hosts, you ministers of His, who do His pleasure.

112. What do Christians pray for in the fourth petition?

In the fourth petition (which is, *Give us this day our daily bread.*[1]) Christians pray that of God's free gift they may receive a competent portion of the good things of this life, and enjoy His blessing with them.[2]

1. *Matthew 6:11*
2. *Proverbs 30:8-9* Remove falsehood and lies far from me; give me neither poverty nor riches—feed me with the food You prescribe for me; ⁹Lest I be full and deny You, and say, Who is the LORD? Or lest I be poor and steal, and profane the name of my God.

   1 Timothy 4:4-5 For every creature of God is good, and nothing is to be refused if it is received with thanksgiving; ⁵for it is sanctified by the word of God and prayer.

   Psalm 90:17 And let the beauty of the LORD our God be upon us, and establish the work of our hands for us; yes, establish the work of our hands.

113. What do Christians pray for in the fifth petition?

In the fifth petition (which is, *And forgive us our debts, as we forgive our debtors*¹) Christians pray that God, for Christ's sake, would freely pardon all their sins;² which they are the more readily encouraged to ask, because by His grace they are enabled from the heart to forgive others.³

1. *Matthew 6:12*
2. *Psalm 51:1-2, 7, 9* Have mercy upon me, O God, according to Your lovingkindness; according to the multitude of Your tender mercies, blot out my transgressions. ²Wash me thoroughly from my iniquity, and cleanse me from my sin. ⁷Purge me with hyssop, and I shall be clean; wash me, and I shall be whiter than snow. ⁹Hide Your face from my sins, and blot out all my iniquities.

   Daniel 9:17-19 Now therefore, our God, hear the prayer of Your servant, and his supplications, and for the Lord's sake cause Your face to shine on Your sanctuary, which is desolate. ¹⁸O my God, incline Your ear and hear; open Your eyes and see our desolations, and the city which is called by Your name; for we do not present our supplications before You because of our righteous deeds, but because of Your great mercies. ¹⁹O Lord, hear! O Lord, forgive! O Lord, listen and act! Do not delay for Your own sake, my God, for Your city and Your people are called by Your name.
3. *Luke 11:4a* And forgive us our sins, for we also forgive everyone who is indebted to us.

   Matthew 18:35 So My heavenly Father also will do to you if each of you, from his heart, does not forgive his brother his trespasses.

114. What do Christians pray for in the sixth petition?

In the sixth petition (which is, *And do not lead us into temptation, but deliver us from the evil one*¹) Christians pray that God would either keep them from being tempted to sin,² or support and deliver them when they are tempted.³

1. *Matthew 6:13a*
2. *Matthew 26:41* Watch and pray, lest you enter into temptation. The spirit indeed is willing, but the flesh is weak.

   Psalm 19:13 Keep back Your servant also from presumptuous sins; let them not have dominion over me. Then I shall be blameless, and I shall be innocent of great transgression.
3. *Psalm 51:10, 12* Create in me a clean heart, O God, and renew a steadfast spirit within me. ¹²Restore to me the joy of Your salvation, and uphold me with Your generous Spirit.

115. What does the conclusion of the Lord's prayer teach His disciples?

The conclusion of the Lord's prayer (which is, *For Yours is the kingdom and the power and the glory forever. Amen*[1]) teaches His disciples to take their encouragement in prayer from God only,[2] and in their prayers to praise Him; ascribing kingdom, power, and glory to Him;[3] and in testimony of their desire and assurance to be heard, to say, Amen.[4]

1. *Matthew 6:13b*
2. *Daniel 9:4,7-9, 16-19* And I prayed to the LORD my God, and made confession, and said, O Lord, great and awesome God, who keeps His covenant and mercy with those who love Him, and with those who keep His commandments. ⁷O Lord, righteousness belongs to You, but to us shame of face, as it is this day—to the men of Judah, to the inhabitants of Jerusalem and all Israel, those near and those far off in all the countries to which You have driven them, because of the unfaithfulness which they have committed against You. ⁸O Lord, to us belongs shame of face, to our kings, our princes, and our fathers, because we have sinned against You. ⁹To the Lord our God belong mercy and forgiveness, though we have rebelled against Him. ¹⁶O Lord, according to all Your righteousness, I pray, let Your anger and Your fury be turned away from Your city Jerusalem, Your holy mountain; because for our sins, and for the iniquities of our fathers, Jerusalem and Your people have become a reproach to all who are around us. ¹⁷Now therefore, our God, hear the prayer of Your servant, and his supplications, and for the Lord's sake cause Your face to shine on Your sanctuary, which is desolate. ¹⁸O my God, incline Your ear and hear; open Your eyes and see our desolations, and the city which is called by Your name; for we do not present our supplications before You because of our righteous deeds, but because of Your great mercies. ¹⁹O Lord, hear! O Lord, forgive! O Lord, listen and act! Do not delay for Your own sake, my God, for Your city and Your people are called by Your name.
3. *1 Chronicles 29:10-13* Therefore David blessed the LORD before all the congregation; and David said: Blessed are You, LORD God of Israel, our Father, forever and ever. ¹¹Yours, O LORD, is the greatness, the power and the glory, the victory and the majesty; for all that is in heaven and in earth is Yours; Yours is the kingdom, O LORD, and You are exalted as head over all. ¹²Both riches and honor come from You, and You reign over all. In Your hand is power and might; in Your hand it is to make great and to give strength to all. ¹³Now therefore, our God, we thank You and praise Your glorious name.

   Revelation 4:11 You are worthy, O Lord, to receive glory and honor and power; for You created all things, and by Your will they exist and were created.
4. *1 Corinthians 14:16* Otherwise, if you bless with the spirit, how will he who occupies the place of the uninformed say Amen at your giving of thanks, since he does not understand what you say?

   Revelation 22:20 He who testifies to these things says, Surely I am coming quickly. Amen. Even so, come, Lord Jesus!

The Shorter Catechism: A Baptist Version

Design & Composition by Simpson Graphics
Printing by BookMasters
On 12 pt. C1S with film lamination and 70# text